PROFESSIONAL SUCCESS

How to Thrive in the Professional World

John M. Latta, CPA, CMC

Windrose Press
San Carlos, California

Published by:
Windrose Press
A division of Orion Group LLC
Post Office Box 790
San Carlos, CA 94070

www.windrosepress.com

Publisher's Cataloging-in-Publication Data
Latta, John M.
   Professional success : how to thrive in the
professional world / John M. Latta.
   p. cm.
   LCCN 2003099056
   ISBN 0-9746591-5-0

   1. Career development. 2. Professional employees.
3. Success in business. I. Title.

HF5381.L3425 2004   650.1
                            QBI03-200955

Disclaimer

Contents

About the Author

John Latta provides business and financial advice to professional firms in Northern California. His clients currently

 include professionals who manage money, practice law, deliver marketing and advertising support, and provide scientific services.

Previously, as a member of the senior management team of Grant Thornton LLP, John was involved in virtually every aspect of the firm's operations including the management of clients, recruiting of personnel, integration of smaller firm mergers, assessment of operating office performance, and teaching and managing professional education programs. His last assignment was as the managing partner of Grant's two San Francisco Bay Area offices.

Early in his career, John's responsibilities for recruiting and managing entry-level personnel aroused his interest in the start-up period for staff and the things they encountered that facilitated and retarded their ability to become productive as rapidly as possible. He has surveyed many young professionals to further expand his understanding of their issues and how these issues are changing within the rapidly evolving professional communities of the 21st century.

Apart from his business of helping professional firms thrive and grow, John can usually be found on or around the water. He serves as a trustee of the San Francisco Maritime National Park Association and is an active member of the century-old Dolphin Swimming & Boating Club, located on San Francisco's Fisherman's Wharf, where he teaches the club's rowing course.

Acknowledgements

Many people, both within the professions and without, have contributed to this book. Some did so through active participation in the project while others generously shared their experiences with me over the years. It would be impossible to acknowledge and thank them all personally.

Several of them stand out, however, as a result of having devoted their valuable time to reading and critiquing the text. A few even endured several iterations of this particular sacrifice as I responded to their ideas with additional material. In particular, this group includes Catherine Kennington, Jeremy Evard, and Catherine Wietholter Evard (who not only shared her observations on the text but also produced the book's killer illustrations), and my colleague Vic Downing of Global Advantage, Inc. Thank you all for your hard work.

A few others also stand out because of their contributions over the years to whatever wisdom finds its way into these pages. This group includes Larry A. Jobe, mentor and partner; L. Paden Neeley, professor extraordinaire and very good friend; and Michael Wolff, who succeeded me as Grant Thornton's National Director of Tax Services. It also includes two truly professional tax professionals who always found ways to bring me back to reality when necessary, Gail Wills and David Ehrhardt. Thank you all for your wisdom and your contributions to my own professional career.

Still others were directly involved in the production of the book, and it would not have been possible without them. They include editor Pam Geisinger and designer Jami Spittler of Jamison Design. I also received invaluable advice from Kathryn Eustis, with whom I've worked in the past on several other publication projects. Thank you all for your very professional services.

All of these contributions would be for naught were it not for the inspiration, patience, and encouragement of my life partner, Martha Tim Lasseter Latta. Thanks here, while clearly required, are so totally inadequate for her role in this project and in my life.

|

—

Success

A successful career as a professional person is as sweet as it gets! After all, what's not to like? You work at the leading edge of a highly sophisticated body of knowledge, help others with things that are really important to them, enjoy the respect of your community, and earn a comfortable, and sometimes very generous, income. Whether your profession is the law or consulting, accounting or architecture, or any of several other important disciplines, you stand on the threshold of a highly satisfying and rewarding career. Now it's up to you to build your personal opportunity into a career that will yield these rewards and more.

Not everyone will succeed, however. Pitfalls abound. The world you are about to enter is tough and demanding. Hours will be long, developing your skills while serving clients can be a real challenge, and success or failure can often be determined by knowledge that isn't taught in professional schools or tested on licensing exams. Having as much information as possible about the environment you're entering—what works and what doesn't, how to grow with your firm, and how to maximize your efforts and your hours—can make a huge difference. It can, indeed, mean the difference between success and failure.

That's what this book is all about. What you'll read here comes from years of observing recent graduates of professional schools as they enter the professional services world and experience the thrills and trials of their first few years—a time when the foundation of success or failure is laid down. Their individual and collective experiences, their responses to recent surveys, and my numerous conversations with them over the years all come together here to provide you with important suggestions. The information in this book can boost you over many of the barriers inherent in these years and help you set the stage for the professional career you seek, a career that will fully justify the investment you've made in your education.

The good news is that a solid understanding of your new surroundings can make a big difference. In a fast-moving environment, a good start is imperative to long-term success. Stumbling out of the starting gate can result in perceptions of you that can end your career before it really begins. Now you can gain important understanding of many of the things about your profession that are simply not covered in most professional curricula. This book will guide you through three essential areas—your new environment, how to manage your own career, and, perhaps most often neglected, how to manage your life as a professional.

In the first of these parts, you'll find a discussion of what the "professions" are all about, what they offer you and your colleagues, and what they offer the public. Learn why they are important to society. This will be followed by an inside look at some realities of how professional firms operate and a discussion of the critical factors that help them thrive or, occasionally, fail. How you respond to these realities and how you contribute to your firm's critical success factors will say a lot about your value and therefore your long-term potential. Some of the things that greatly frustrate your entry-level colleagues will roll off your back because you'll understand their causes and appreciate their significance. You'll be better able to keep your eye on the ball.

The second part will help you put your own career development in perspective and then go about its management with confidence and consistency. You are the responsible party here. No one else can do it for you, and you should gladly and enthusiastically manage your own career. In these chapters, you'll find helpful information on a variety of key elements—managing your time and your relationships, taking a role in marketing and selling the services of your firm, and finding a mentoring relationship, which can be a valuable thing for both the mentor and the protégé. You'll also learn the value of compounding your present knowledge by learning an entirely new discipline.

Engaged as you will be in an exciting and challenging career, the career for which you've been eagerly preparing for several years, it will be surprisingly easy for you to forget or neglect the other important things in life. Families and friends balance our professional lives and, in the end result for most of us, are central to why we dedicate ourselves to our careers. Good habits surrounding this dedication to families and friends can yield rich rewards later in our careers, not to speak of our lives.

So can good money management habits, and you'll find here some very specific suggestions in this regard. The most consistently noted problem of early-career professionals involves personal money management. At a time when they are making more money than they've ever made in their lives, they often aren't quite sure what to do with it all. They find themselves with large and expensive credit card debt and without what they consider to be basic necessities. This chapter can help.

In addition, several other important topics addressed—such as professional and business ethics and personal communication skills—will round out your view of the challenge ahead and the environment in which you will be pursuing that challenge. Another chapter will help you better understand your relationship with your firm, and how to view that as a partnership in which both parties can thrive and prosper through combined efforts.

So congratulations on taking an important step in building a successful career as a professional. Your investment in this book will provide you with many of the tools that you'll need. We'd love to know your thoughts and opinions as you complete your reading and put the things you'll have learned to work. Please visit our website at www.windrosepress.com and share your experiences with us. If you would like to participate in our future surveys of early career professionals, please let us know how we can contact you.

Best wishes for professional success!

2

What is a "Professional" Anyway?

The word "professional" conveys a certain enduring quality that, in my book, makes it a very special word. "Professional football," for example, represents the state of the art. A person's performance, in whatever endeavor, is described as "professional" when it reaches that special level of excellence so as to be truly admirable. And to note that someone is a "professional person" is to convey a distinction about that person's character and other qualities related to education and commitment to the community. In short, being thought of as a professional is a special type of recognition from which most of us gain a great deal of personal satisfaction, before we even begin to talk about the rewards of serving others, mixing with interesting colleagues, and earning a superior income from our work. So what is being a professional all about? To understand the answer to that, we will begin with the way in which the professions are practiced.

Professional firms are different from any other type of business that a new university graduate might have the opportunity to work for. They share similarities with other service businesses in that they are organized around a profit motive and exist to serve their clientele. But they also serve a different master—they serve their communities and, more tangibly, the regulatory and ethical requirements imposed upon them. They are not unlike some not-for-profit organizations in their public responsibility and service elements, and yet many professional service firms are very profitable for their owners. In fact, the prospect of generous income brings a lot of bright people into the professions each year. This profit motive places professional firms squarely into the business environment even though they don't generally carry inventory or (until recently) list their ownership rights in public markets.

In a recent article, William F. Ezzel, Chairman of the American Institute of Certified Public Accountants, described his profession in this way:

"We are a *profession*, not a trade. Consequently, we have responsibilities not limited to but certainly including

- An unwavering commitment to a code of ethics.

- A distinct and evolving body of knowledge.

- A sense of duty to the public interest.

- Standards of excellence.

- A shared sense of purpose.

It is vital that our clients, our employers, our employees, our students and our colleagues appreciate us not just as individuals, but collectively—as a profession."

(Journal of Accountancy, February, 2003, p.58)

Members of the "recognized" professions deliver their services from a platform of dedication to their communities, and indeed to the community at large, that sets them apart from other business men and women. An attorney, a professional engineer, a certified public accountant, an architect—each of these individuals ordinarily represents a community member who is well-educated and who, as part and parcel of his business, manifests a commitment to his community in response to the community's need for his intelligence, objectivity, skills, and breadth of vision. In short, he builds his business around the interests of the community. For the most part, the community responds by treating him with that special level of respect reserved for its highly valued members.

What are the "Recognized" Professions?

For purposes of this book, and I believe for general understanding as well, the "recognized professions" are those service careers that share the following characteristics:

- They involve complex bodies of esoteric knowledge not readily accessible by the general public. I want my surgeon, for example, to know as much as possible about all of my contiguous parts and their inner workings before opening up any one of them.

- Their knowledge base is continually changing and evolving. Whether it's the judicial evolution of a body of law, the findings of new medical research, or legislated changes in the tax code, staying on top of these changes is critical.

- Their practice requires highly specialized, often graduate-level, education. Total immersion in the required subject matter, under the guidance of the already educated, is usually the most efficient way to impart the required knowledge in students of the profession.

- Their practice usually has societal implications. The fair and competent administration of the law, for example, is critical to the efficient functioning of our communities, just as the design of an office tower must assure that it doesn't collapse and endanger the public.

- They usually require governmental certification that often necessitates an internship period to assure that the individual develops experience and delivery skills before he is permitted to serve the public without supervision.

- Their practitioners are generally respected by the community for these characteristics, and therefore enjoy a unique status within it.

This book is directed at those seeking to practice in the professions and particularly those at firms that regularly hire fresh-from-the-campus graduates every year. The largest of these professions, and therefore where the thrust of this book is directed, are accounting, consulting, and law. Others might include actuarial, architecture, engineering, and some professional financial services. Generally, the medical and dental professions are not practiced in the types of firms that are the focus of this book, and they have such unique characteristics that they are not specifically addressed.

But that said, many of the dynamics that you'll read about here will also apply to many other career paths as well. In a broader sense, therefore, this book is for all who are about to finish their formal education and enter the job market for the first time.

Need Satisfaction in the Professions

So what is it about these particular occupations that draw people into them? I believe one of the strongest attractions is the opportunity to serve others. Most of the really outstanding professionals I've run across in my career derive a deep satisfaction from this opportunity. The chance to truly help others solve their life's problems, to clear away obstacles, or to help them more effectively pursue their goals has always struck me as a key driver for most of the professionals I've personally used in my life, along with many others who have been my partners and employees.

Now, there's a touchy-feely sort of sound to what I've just written that many people might reject. So let me elaborate. The professions that are the focus of this book are not public charities, and their partners are not social workers. Most are all business, and some are even downright insensitive to the feelings of their clients. So this is not about warm and fuzzy, and it's not about political correctness. Instead, it is about the "high" that most of us feel when a client brings us an important problem and we solve it—competently, efficiently, and with a style that says to anyone who might be watching, "I am a professional." It may also be about the personal, soft side of the relationship, but that's not the core of the issue. What it is about is solving a problem that's important to someone else, and the bigger the problem the better. I have had no greater rush in my career than the times when I've done that really well.

Being on the Cutting Edge

Another element that I believe drives most professionals, particularly the good ones, is the desire to stay on the cutting edge of an esoteric and complex body of knowledge. It has to be. If it were otherwise, our courts would be packed (even more than now) with professional service failures. And the few professionals who did consistently manage to stay ahead of the game would be unaffordable. As it is, considering the unimaginable complexity of most bodies of professional knowledge, and the huge numbers of consumers served by these professions, there are surprisingly few real failures of the system.

The reason that the system works as well as it does, it seems to me, is that professionals by and large are really turned on by the changing landscape of their professions. This element, which wasn't much of a factor in the nineteenth and early twentieth centuries, has become a real draw for those of us who choose to hold ourselves out as having a specialized way of helping others. It's a part of the public respect aspect of our lives, to be sure, but it's much more. Perhaps it's a macho thing (what's the female of macho?), but a part of our self-identity involves this particular type of strength and vitality. Maybe it's the twenty-first century version of drilling sixteen tons of #9 coal.

Being in on What's Happening

Another driver for many of us is the desire to be at the center of things. Many professionals have an active involvement with their clients only when something important is going on. A corporation decides to build its own building or campus. A company needs to upgrade its existing software system to compete. Or an investor tallies up her taxes at year end for Uncle Sam. These events are usually quite significant to those experiencing them. They oftentimes represent important crossroads for the people and the organizations involved. If you are the professional practitioner called in to assist, then you are at the center of major decision-making activity. The feeling of importance that comes with that often provides one with a great deal of inner satisfaction, however superficial that might seem.

Being in a Community of Professionals

Most professional communities are challenging places–intellectually challenging, and also competitively stimulating. They can be tough places. Any collection of professionals who place great value on such fundamental elements as quality, precision, and knowledge are apt to be pretty unforgiving. And no sin is quite as unforgivable as ignorant error. This makes staying at the top of the game pretty important.

Each of these communities will usually have, and almost always recognize, a very small number of members who possess clearly superior technical knowledge. While every member would aspire to be recognized for this level of knowledge, it's not required. But anyone who seems to be anchoring the other end of the spectrum with marginal or clearly deficient technical knowledge will be shunned. This makes membership in any community of professionals challenging. To those who stay for a career, that atmosphere is a stimulating challenge, but it is usually too stressful for those who aren't positively motivated by that competition.

Assessing What This Holds for You

Most of the thousands of university graduates who enter the professions each year have no real basis to assess their suitability for a career there. By their fifth or so year of work, almost all will have formed a strong opinion about whether they chose the right career. In between, they've had a variety of experiences that have influenced this opinion. Many will have left the profession altogether at this point. Many will have changed firms. Some will have made these decisions wisely and some not so wisely because of anecdotal experiences that have pushed them in one particular direction. My experience has taught me that young professionals' decisions to stay with it or get out can easily be made for the wrong reasons.

A professional career can be a very rewarding thing to experience, both in terms of inner satisfaction and financial rewards. It can also be a high-pressure hell if those psychic rewards don't do it for you. The decision to make it a career or look elsewhere for your future can best be made by continually measuring the costs against the fundamental payoffs that your profession offers. Whatever criteria that you may apply in assessing your professional career (and several are suggested in this book), I would encourage you to look through your day-to-day experiences over these first few years and measure your own payoff against your frustrations. Liking the basic rewards that your profession offers will help a great deal in getting you through the trials of your early years such as the frustrations of the scheduling game where you always seem to be the loser, or the guy you work for who knows it all but can't manage his way to the restroom.

If your profession continually comes up short in this comparison, then recognize that you've had a few years of wonderfully diverse real-world growth, and don't hesitate to go out and find a way to put all you've learned to work somewhere else.

3

Some Realities of
Professional Firms

A professional firm is very much a business. Its success
depends at least as much on its effective operation as on
discharging its professional responsibilities. This chapter
is about the organization of a professional firm–how it
serves its clients and makes money doing it and how it dis-
tributes the money it makes.

Many of the traditional rules of professional firm ownership and organization have become quite blurry in recent
years. Some professions have begun accepting non-mem-
bers as firm owners. Attorneys are now in partnership with
accountants and even professional engineers. Consulting
firms are being bought by technology product companies.
Accounting firms are being acquired by major financial
service providers to serve as feeders for future consumers of
their financial products. These anomalies will probably
continue to grow in the search for greater and greater
internal and market efficiencies.

People as the Machinery of Production

One of the most important drivers behind the environment that you will encounter in the professional world is
the simple fact that you and all of your colleagues are the
machinery of production. No manufacturing plant yet
exists that can defend a client in the courtroom, manage an
investment portfolio, or design a new office tower. These
things, for the present at least, must be done by people.
Yet the process by which they are completed often closely
resembles a manufacturing operation with all its interde-
pendencies and timing issues. A firm's employees, therefore, are not only its "product", but its production machinery as well.

This basic fact leads to several considerations that will
have a direct impact on you. Understanding them is essential to preparing yourself for what you will experience in
this new environment. Picture yourself as a key machine on
a typical manufacturing production line. What would you
be expected to do with your day?'Well, first, you would be
expected to be as productive as possible when on-line, and

to stay on-line as much as possible. In fact, if you could work extra hours in a day, another shift for example, so much the better. This defines the concept of utilization, which we'll talk about more in the following chapter.

Well, you say, you are not a machine and this is not a production line–or is it? Your employer would likely be astute enough not to describe you as such, yet many policies and procedures will look to you as though that is exactly the way he sees it. This circumstance alone accounts for many of the difficulties you will encounter in the transition from campus to real world.

You are the machinery of production. If you are off-line or are not as productive as possible, your employer suffers the consequences. Other parts of the process might slow as a result. If your "station" produces an unacceptably high defect rate, the process has to be halted in order to recycle the reject product. In the professional environment, time is money in a very real sense. It is the only product that a professional firm has to sell. Consequently, in most professions there is tremendous pressure to be on-line for as many hours during the day as possible, and often in fact more than a normal day, and to be at least as productive as everyone else, and to not slow the process through inefficient or defective workmanship. Sound like a high-pressure environment? It certainly can be.

In some professions, and indeed some firms, this pressure is more intense than in others. And some professions and firms are better than others at helping their personnel deal with the resulting stress. The fact, however, is that the high-pressure world of professional services is a vastly different world than the university campus. You will be on-line all day, every day, and will be expected to devote significant chunks of your personal time to the production line whenever required to get the "product" out the door. In surveys I've done, the resulting pressure is one of the most often mentioned difficulties in transitioning from campus to the world of professional services.

Partners and Everyone Else

In most of the professions, the majority of firms are managed as partnerships, the traditional form of organization. The principal exception is found in a few mega-size accounting and consulting organizations that tend to be run as hierarchies. More on them later.

Increasingly, many professional firms are called professional corporations, limited liability companies, or limited liability partnerships as a result of their legal status, but the fact is that the traditional partnership organization still governs how most of them are actually operated. This is because the partnership culture generally supplies the right model for organizing efficient and productive service. Thus, the partner (who may now be called a "shareholder" or "member") is the key player. For simplicity, we will refer throughout this book to all who are owner-managers of a professional firm as "partners."

The partner's key responsibilities are usually:

- To manage key client relationships and develop new ones;

- To manage the delivery of services to those clients; and

- To manage the staff assigned to deliver those services.

He, and increasingly in recent years she, is the key individual, the point person in the scheme of client service. This person is often, although not always, the most broadly capable individual on the team in terms of the general services being delivered to that client. Other highly specialized technicians will often bring capabilities to the team that supplement the more general skills of the partner and other members. The team, however, will largely be composed of the firm's professional staff–i.e., you and your colleagues.

The partner, then, is ordinarily responsible for the overall service to his or her clients. Thus, she focuses on the top-level technical considerations, on the efficient progress of the assignment, and on maintaining communications with key client personnel. These represent the most valuable components of the services being provided, as well as the maintenance of good client relationships. These, therefore, are where the most competent and experienced individual–in short, the partner–should be focusing his or her attention.

In order for the partner assigned to a particular account to focus only on the high-level aspects of client service, a client service team is usually assembled with firm members of various levels of professional experience and skill. A senior hands-on individual is often assigned to manage the day-to-day progress of the services to that particular client. This person may be called a manager, but in a large client engagement may actually be a less-experienced partner.

A team of employees selected for the appropriateness of their skills and experience will be assembled in support of and report to that individual, for that particular project. Depending upon the profession and the size of the client and project, this team might range anywhere from two or three individuals, including the partner, to several hundred or more. In very large client projects, such as an audit of a Fortune 100 client, or the design of a major new office campus, the team might actually include several partners.

Typically, the non-management-level staff members of a professional firm are pooled until temporarily assigned to a particular project. I say temporarily, but bear in mind that in the case of a very large firm and a very large project, this temporary period might extend into months or even years. Thus, when the project ends, the staff assigned to it will be returned to the pool unless another project, perhaps one that has been on hold pending staff availability, needs additional people.

How Does Your Firm Make its Money?

Professional firms sell time. They sell the time of their partners, but importantly, they also sell the time of their employees. The calculation of the price charged for the time of partners and employees varies considerably from firm to firm, but the basic principle does not. If a firm were to sell the time of its staff members at its cost (salary + benefits + payroll taxes, etc.), then it obviously wouldn't make a profit on that important component of client service. So the firm will establish a billing rate for each member of its staff that is sufficient to cover its costs and to provide a profit on that individual's client service time. While the calculation may differ between professions, and even between firms, a staff person's time will be sold to clients at some multiple of the individual's direct and indirect cost to the firm.

With a few notable exceptions (we'll discuss them later) most large firms make the largest portion of their profits from selling the time of their non-partners. This concept is known as leverage, and its components are the number of staff members the firm is able to productively employ on a given client project, and the degree to which the firm is able to mark up the salary costs of those individuals. The size and complexity of the project governs the number of staff members used, and the market determines the mark up. We'll look closer at leverage in the next chapter.

The degree to which a particular firm emphasizes the amount of its partners' billable client service time will tell you a lot about the organization and operation of that firm. A big firm that provides large-project services for its clients typically won't emphasize the billable time of its partners. Instead, it will rely on its partners to manage client relationships and engagements. This is a very high value role in itself because it facilitates the efficient and profitable delivery of services and puts the partner in a position to identify a continuing stream of opportunities for the firm to sell additional services.

Such firms count on their partners to maintain close relationships with one or more very large clients with very sophisticated needs that can be converted into large projects requiring large numbers of staff. Not everyone can do this. This partner, to be successful, must herself be a very sophisticated professional, probably a very good business person in her own right, who can move in decision-maker circles and command respect from both client and employees.

She will be judged on the amount and profitability of the work that she generates for her firm through her activities and project management. In a very real sense, she is an entrepreneur-manager in her own right, all within the walls of her firm. This model is typically found in the large accounting and consulting firms. In large architecture and engineering firms, there may be little repeat business with a particular client, but projects can be even larger and the basic model is similar. Leverage is high here, perhaps twenty or more non-partners per partner. In this situation, the profitability derived from a particular partner's work usually has little to do with the technical services she personally provides. Instead, it has everything to do with the number of non-partners employed on her projects and the salary multiple that she is able to bill for the work.

The other extreme in terms of leverage can often be found in small, mid-sized, and sometimes even very large law firms. The nature of their services often demands very high levels of technical expertise and experience, and the services are then customized for the needs of a particular client and situation. For example, in negotiating the details of a complex merger, the critical ingredient will likely be the individual partner's many years of experience in this highly specialized area. He carries this capability around in his head, and the opportunity to involve less experienced staff may be limited to very routine and mundane tasks supporting the negotiating partner–basic legal research, for example. In this case, the partner's client service time will usually be quite high, and given the firm's limited opportunity to utilize its staff, so will his billing rate. This is how the firm makes its profit–by providing large amounts of very high value services. Here, the firm's leverage may be quite low by the standards of the accounting and consulting professions. It is not uncommon in this situation to find a ratio of only one staff member or associate per partner, or even fewer. This model might also be found at small boutique firms such as money managers, CPAs, and consultants.

Large law firms are increasingly finding ways to build greater leverage into their practices. As litigation becomes more complex, and cases become larger, these firms are able to more efficiently segment work into subordinate projects that can be assigned to less experienced associates. As in the case of the merger negotiation noted above, the services must still be customized, but this is done by the lead partner, who in turn directs the activities. Obviously, this represents an opportunity to achieve leverage greater than might be possible in a smaller project. This trend is being driven not only by the firms themselves, but also by the clients who are increasingly unwilling to pay for expensive partner time to do the routine work involved in many pieces of large projects.

The Allocation of Firm Profits

So now that you know how a professional firm makes its money, let's look at how its partners all feed from this communal trough. As mentioned above, most professional service firms are partnerships, or at least are operated as such. This happens for a reason, actually several reasons. Number one, professionals almost by definition are independent thinkers who will not readily submit to a typical corporate (read hierarchical) organization with well defined and firmly established lines of reporting. Ordinarily these individuals are highly educated and have learned to think and act for themselves. They don't generally make good foot soldiers. In their professional practices, they want to be impact players. In short, they want to be partners and help call the shots.

Another reason that the partnership form of organization is so common in the professional community lies in the concept of shared resources—support resources to be sure, but also the resources represented by having a group of partners who either do the same thing (as in a boutique practice) or have complementary skills (as in the case of a broad, general practice). Sharing support resources makes sense. In the case of a law firm for example, several senior attorneys will require essentially the same type of support for their individual practices (such as a human resources function or a computer network) but seldom will they need them all of the time. Sharing them reduces costs and is simply more efficient. Further, other partners represent other minds to help think through problems and provide back up for vacations and illnesses.

Most partnerships develop their own unique compensation systems. The universal starting point is the profit for a given period after paying all operating costs and expenses. This profit is the property of the partners as a group. The devil is in the details, as they say, and the method of splitting this profit among those partners is typically unique to the partnership, and is almost always the subject of discussion, frustration, complaints, and periodic reexamination.

Ideally, the partnership will have developed a set of criteria that, when combined with the wisdom and judgment of one or more of its key members, will result in some quasi-empirical evaluation of each partner's individual contribution to earning the year's profit. This in turn will prescribe the portion of the pie that each partner will be allocated for the year, or perhaps for the coming period. Now remember, I said ideally. The large consulting and CPA firms, for example, have elaborate means of measuring the various elements of partner performance deemed by them to be important to present and future profitability. These systems then become the basis of distributing firm profits, and sometimes involve bonuses that are actually charged to the firm as an expense before annual profit is determined. Conventional wisdom generally holds that you get what you choose to measure, and therefore these systems are thought to represent the best one can do with a very difficult challenge in a highly charged environment. Whether they actually produce a better result is often questionable.

Other factors sometimes taken into account in determining the profit allocation can include seniority, local cost of living differences (in the case of firms with multiple locations), and individual need. At best, most systems of partner profit allocation constitute "rough justice," and this one element of partnership operations probably accounts for more failed partnerships than any other, as you might imagine. People seldom see the same circumstances in the same way in the highly charged arena of partner compensation.

The Client Relationship Manager

One can argue that the most important role within any professional firm is that of client relationship manager. The title of this function varies considerably from profession to profession and firm to firm, but the role is essentially the same in all. This person is the one individual who has the ultimate responsibility for the services provided to, the profitability of, and ultimately the happiness of and continued relationship with a particular client. For most clients, particularly the larger ones, this role will almost always be that of a partner.

Over the last two decades or so, the title of partner has increasingly been awarded to many other types of players in the professional firm, so it can no longer be assumed that a particular partner's job is to manage a group of clients. Also, in many firms today, the firm's smaller or more highly specialized clients are assigned to non-partners, thus further diluting the meaning of the title. But no matter, the role of client relationship manager—the person ultimately responsible for satisfying the needs of a client—whatever it might be called, is arguably the most satisfying responsibility in the professional world. It is the holy grail of professionalism.

I vividly remember the occasion of my first having this responsibility. It came in my third year as a tax specialist, and resulted from the retirement of a very senior partner from active practice. His clients were divided up among several of us. The few who came my way were clearly the ones that nobody really cared if we retained or lost, and I even knew that at the time. But knowing it didn't lessen the experience in the slightest. The thrill of first being the main man will be with me forever. Since then, I've legitimately come by that responsibility many times (by bringing clients to the firm), but none of those later experiences, which usually involved clients much more important than that first meager collection, were any sweeter.

This first collection of throw-away clients was highly educational for me and beneficial to my career. From them, I became comfortable with the responsibility of assuring that their technical needs were met competently and professionally, and that they were happy with the service. There I first realized that those two objectives do not always go hand in hand; that on occasion you can do the right thing and have, in fact, a very unhappy client. The tax consultant is not always the bearer of good news. Here, I first confronted the professional dilemma that can result from the always present, but sometimes conflicting, goals of technical excellence and client service. I strongly recommend that you seek the responsibility as early as possible in your career. Here is a really important payoff of being a professional.

Some Partners are More Equal Than Others

Several trends have merged in recent years to cause the creation of, how shall we say it, a second class of partner, often referred to as a non-equity partner. This position was created in response to competitive pressures and the need to keep happy key employees who for whatever reason might not be afforded the opportunity to become partners. Perhaps an employee is a highly focused technical specialist who lacks the relationship management skills to be responsible for key clients or a large staff of broadly based professionals. Perhaps he just happens to be in a firm or office where there are already too many partners for the profit pool.

A variety of reasons, often having no negative implications upon the person himself, can account for a partnership position not being available to a highly valued senior level employee. A non-equity partner position provides a way to demonstrate the firm's commitment to and belief in this person without diluting its partner base, or promoting someone whose skills, however valuable, aren't compatible with the firm's partner guidelines.

In most cases, the distinction between one class of partner and another is purely internal. The non-equity partner presents himself to the world simply as a partner. That's how his business card reads and that's ordinarily how his written communications present him. Thus, from the standpoint of the status of partnership, he enjoys it in full outside the firm. Often, no one inside the firm except the partner group sees any distinction either.

Another way that the non-equity partner position has been used in recent years, is to promote a key employee to the partnership on a trial basis. The key expectation here is that satisfactory performance as a non-equity partner will be rewarded by promotion to full partner after a certain period. Sometimes, this is actually accompanied by an "up or out" policy under which no one is permitted to make a career as a non-equity partner. This is just the opposite of the high-level technician noted above whose non-equity partner status is often, by definition, a career position.

Whichever the situation, you can be assured that a non-equity partner is someone the firm values quite highly—and wants the world to value as well.

4

You and Your Firm's Success

A good many of the unique characteristics that you will encounter in your firm will result from the nature of the business of professional services. Perhaps you will have to share an office or cubicle with another junior staff person. Or you may chafe under the deadlines for reporting your time, or be frustrated by reimbursement policies that don't allow you to be reimbursed for out-of-pocket business expenses until the next month. Understand the business of professional services and you will at least have the background for many of these frustrations.

Cash Flow is King

The place to start to understand our business is with the subject of cash flow. Most manufacturing and transportation companies are all about capital investment and capacity. The technology world is about staying ahead of the curve and market share. Professional firms, on the other hand, are all about cash flow. Our firms don't typically have large asset bases like United Airlines or General Motors. And while staying ahead of the knowledge curve is certainly essential, the curve is not nearly so steep as in other industries, and staying ahead is largely a matter of individual effort. Rather, the thing your firm has to do to be successful (among others admittedly) is to create and manage its cash flow.

Think about it. Your firm's largest cost of doing business is you—you and your colleagues that is. Staff salary costs typically soak up somewhere between one-third and half of the revenue generated by the firm. As we'll explore later, managing that huge monthly cost is often marked by periods of under-utilization of personnel (read, "no revenue coming in").

Next is the landlord's cut of the pie, which is so costly that it is often quoted as a price per square foot of space per month. The monthly cost for each of those small pieces of shelter can run upward of $4 or $5 in major metropolitan areas. Considering that it usually takes somewhere around 200 square feet to support just one employee, rent is often a substantial cost of doing business, which explains a lot about why many large firms in recent years have moved decisively in the direction of office hoteling, or the sharing of office or cubicle space among several employees who are not regularly in the office at the same time, and toward encouraging employees to work at home.

Look around and you will see a number of other elements of your firm's operations that also continually require considerable resources—computers and related software, continuing education for you and your colleagues, reference resources, travel, and on and on.

The common element inherent in virtually all of these costs is that they relate rather directly to the firm's monthly revenue, and they must be paid monthly. They do not represent assets that can be financed by long-term borrowing. Thus, the cash flow generated by the services that you and others provide your firm's clients is critically important to keeping the doors open month-to-month. And the partners don't get to eat until you and the landlord and the other vendors get your cut first. That's what being a partner means on a very practical level. In contracting for your services, the firm's partners have not only provided their personal guarantees that you and these others will be paid, but have also subordinated their own livelihoods to those payments. Think they are not interested in the firm's cash flow? Think again!

Managing Costs and Profits

So just how do your partners manage the economics of the practice in order to have some assurance that they will also be able to eat? It all begins with what the firm charges its clients for the services that you and your colleagues provide. This is almost universally done, in one way or another, on an hourly basis. Most firms have a formula for converting their salary costs into a desired billing rate per hour of time devoted to client work. This may be on an individual basis or for an entire job classification. Or it might be a standard charge for a particular team or type of project. Sometimes, the unit of measure is not hours but days or even weeks. This depends largely on the size of the projects typically performed by the firm.

The firm that I was a part of for many years computed this on an individual hourly basis, giving consideration to such factors as desired profitability per employee and the amount of down time typical for each particular employee class. Thus, for a particular class of employee, the hourly billing rate might be set at, say, 4% of monthly salary. If the employee's base salary happened to be $48,000 per year, then the hourly standard rate for that employee would be $160 per hour ($48,000 / 12 x .04). This rate often varied between two employees at the same salary level but in different divisions. In one, the typical staff member was expected to charge clients for around 1,800 hours annually. This person's counterpart in another division, because of the nature of the required work, anticipated only 1,400 hours. The second person's rate was calculated to take this lower chargeability into account, and as a result was correspondingly higher. Obviously, as employees advanced in responsibility, and therefore salary, their associated hourly billing rates advanced as well.

The ultimate test of the appropriateness of the firm's billing rates is in the hands of an outsider, namely the client. This is the person who ultimately determines whether the rates make sense by what she will pay for a given service. Many professions, particularly in areas where the outcome of the work is unknown when a project is begun, have figured out that services that produce highly satisfactory results, are worth more than other services, even when both are performed by the same individual. Thus, "value billing" has gained some currency in recent years.

Sometimes value billing takes the form of the firm charging one rate for a particular type of service, and another, higher rate for another. This might happen where the firm possesses a particularly unique skill set in a competitive environment where no one else has experience to match. Other times it may take the form of an upfront agreement with the client that if the outcome is "A," then the fee will be based on the firm's standard fee schedule, but if the outcome is "A++," then the related fee will be at a higher, negotiated rate. This arrangement might be used, for example, by a consultant who has been retained by his client to negotiate favorable terms with a rate-setting agency.

The fee for a large, multi-year project will often be negotiated during the bidding process and then forgotten except at the project management level for the duration of the project. In this situation, an entry-level staff person may not even know how her own services contribute to the revenue stream of the firm. And in fact it may not even be possible to calculate this until the project has been completed.

Leverage and Utilization

These concepts were introduced earlier, but deserve mention again because of their importance. These two variables are often the most important determinates of firm profitability, particularly in larger firms. And here is where you will find the source of many of the pressures that you will likely experience in the professional world.

"Leverage" defines the degree to which non-partner staff can be employed on a given project, and more broadly in a given firm. As noted above, firms that ordinarily perform very large projects for their (usually very large) clients make their money off of the markup of staff costs. The responsible partner may not personally charge any client service time to the project at all, but may confine his or her time to maintaining the client relationship and to assuring that the project is properly staffed and managed. Consequently, the more non-partners (whose salary costs are usually fixed at a certain level) who can be employed on a project, the greater the project's profitability. Likewise, the larger total number of staff that a firm can employ, and keep productively engaged in servicing clients (a big "if"), the greater will be its profitability.

And herein lies the catch. The firm needs for its staff to be as large as possible when it charges its clients, but as small as possible on payday. Said another way, it wants to maintain just barely enough staff to do the work, but never more than it needs. Or still another way, if its staff is too small (or composed of people with the wrong skills), then it will have difficulty completing projects on a timely basis. But if it has too many people (or, again, people with the wrong skills), then it will be paying for skills that it cannot employ. Either way, it loses.

As you might imagine, projects come and they go; sometimes they come simultaneously, and sometimes there is no work at all. Some projects require one particular skill in abundance, and others require different skills altogether. Consequently, achieving just the right balance through staff scheduling is often very challenging. It is an art, not a science. And thus, you may find yourself working "24/7" for a long period followed by another period "on the beach," or without any client assignment at all. And during the 24/7 period, you may find that your colleague who is carrying half of the load at your level is pulled off to help complete a totally different project, effectively doubling your workload. It's all about staff mix and leverage.

Utilization is the other key component of profitability. This term defines the degree to which you and your fellow staff members are busy actually servicing clients. Obviously, the greater your utilization in a given period, the greater the fees, and all else being equal, the better the chance that the partners' children will have a Santa visit this year. All else is not ordinarily equal, however. Overtime pay or bonuses reduce the profitability of a project, and the firm pays other out-of-pocket costs in supporting your long hours. If the leverage is also high, the margin (project profitability as a percent of the related fees) will be slightly reduced, but it will still be very good even after these extra costs.

As you might now imagine, your firm will seek to keep you working on client projects as much as possible (just short of burning you out), and as consistently throughout the year as possible. To restate the obvious, scheduling is an art and not a science. The timing of client projects is very seldom within the complete control of the firm. Courts set trial dates, SEC reports are due when they are due, corporate acquisitions happen when the parties decide to negotiate them, and so on. The skill involved in scheduling, particularly in large consulting and accounting firms, is often underappreciated. Efficient scheduling can be a critical determinate of firm profitability and, by the way, of your career advancement. I'll have more to say about that later.

The Management of Receivables

So it's time for the bill to go out. The partner reviews the time that you and your colleagues have recorded since the last billing, checks the terms in the arrangement letter or contract with the client, prepares and then mails a bill. All finished? Not quite. In some firms, this is only the beginning of the process. The client still has to pay the bill before the cycle is complete and the money's in the bank to pay you, the landlord, and all the others.

"Receivable management" is a general term that relates to the process of collecting amounts owed to the firm by its clients. The practices employed to do this are as varied as the firms themselves. Some professions don't know how good they have it. Money managers, who have direct access to large pools of their clients' money, simply deduct their periodic fees from each client's account–end of cash flow cycle! Most of us are not so fortunate.

At the other extreme are some trial lawyers who, under deferred billing agreements with their clients, might be paid for their services only at the conclusion of the litigation. This can be years! And if the client (or in the client's view, the attorney) loses the case, extracting teeth can look easy compared to getting that bill paid. Further complicating the situation are "contingent" arrangements wherein the attorney will be paid only out of the client's award if the litigation is successful. Fortunately, these practices are becoming rarer as attorneys find more creative ways to work with their clients and manage their cash flow.

For those of us who do not function at either of these extremes, the billing is followed by a period of waiting for the client to pay. Many factors can affect the time it takes for this to happen. The first, and often most important, is the payment terms stated in the contract or arrangement letter governing the work. You might think this is the end of the matter, but as you should know by now, people don't always do what they say they will do. Clients have been known to delay the payment of a professional's bill because of some perceived dissatisfaction with the services performed—no matter the contract terms. This is quite common, actually, and points to the value of the partner time devoted to maintenance of good relations and open communication with the client. Identifying problems quickly, and then dealing with them openly and vigorously, can substantially reduce the likelihood of a payment issue arising as a result.

Or the client may be having its own cash flow problems, and while fully intending to pay your firm's bill, it might simply slow the process down a bit to let its own receipts catch up with its bills. In large companies, multiple approvals are sometime required for a large payment. People go on vacation. And, believe it or not, your firm's bills can fall between the cracks— i.e. simply get lost in the payment process.

In addition to the immediate disruption of the cash-flow cycle, another problem arises from overdue payment of the firm's bills. The longer a bill is outstanding, the greater the possibility that it will not be paid in full. As noted, the delay may indicate a service problem that will result in the amount being negotiated down. The individual who approves payments may resign, and her replacement may challenge her predecessor's decisions. And companies develop financial problems that result in creditors being paid only a certain portion of what they're owed. So the goal should always be to collect receivables promptly, and to follow up right away if they're not.

The question, then, is what does your firm (or, most often the partner) do about a slow-paying client? Different people approach this challenge differently. One thing is common, however, among firms that are known for good receivable practices. They have established a culture that says, "Get on it!" In other words, as soon as a payment delay becomes evident, action is taken to address the situation. Perhaps this takes the form of a reminder from the firm's accounting department. Or a staff member might be assigned to contact the client's accounting department to follow up. If these actions are not successful, the partner will get directly involved to turn up the reason for the delay, and to subtly remind the client of its obligation.

Collecting from clients is a critical element in the cash flow cycle that demands continuing awareness and diligent effort. It is one of the areas where the partner earns his money.

5

Who's in Charge of Your Career?

Throughout your formal education, you've been in charge. You selected a major field of study, analyzed the elective courses available to you, and decided how much of yourself to put into them. Your vision of the future guided these choices, and your dedication and performance brought them to life. Now you're about to enter into an entirely new phase in your career. Who will be responsible for these kinds of educational and development decisions from this point on? In short, who's responsible for your career?

The Responsible Party

I've asked this question of a number of professionals in the first years of their careers. Their answers are always interesting and often, in my opinion, misguided. I believe that any answer other than "I am" is wrong. Here's why.

Many professional school graduates, particularly consultants, accountants, and attorneys, will go to work in large firms. Many of these firms have developed very efficient and effective programs for integrating new graduates into their operations. This often includes multi-year, in-house training programs to shepherd their staff through the early years of their careers, often teaching about the firms' own business and the businesses of their clients.

Firms that do not operate their own internal training regimens often budget for external programs to educate their personnel. Many will even pay a part or all of the cost of advanced degrees for staff.

Many firms also go to some lengths to rotate their employees through different types of job assignments in order to help them gain all of the skills that will make them increasingly profitable for the firm.

These substantial investments are often further supported by individual counsel to young staff members on where their careers are headed within the firm and what educational opportunities would be most helpful to their development. Educational options are often included in annual performance reviews and goal setting so as to assure, as much as possible, that project assignment decisions are made with consideration for acquired knowledge.

Most firms' partners take a genuine interest in employees' career development. Partners often dedicate a portion of their time each year to teaching in firm training programs. The interaction with staff is important to them, and they get great satisfaction from contributing to the career development of young professionals.

Sounds ideal. And in many ways it is. So with such an impressive array of career guidance and educational opportunities provided for you, why do I so emphatically feel that you must be, and importantly, must see yourself as being, responsible for your own career development? Three reasons.

First, as well-intentioned as their efforts may be, these firms don't have to live with the results! That is, their future doesn't depend on your personal career development. But yours does. They will likely say (and genuinely believe) that their future does indeed depend on their success in developing the careers of all of their professional personnel. I would be surprised if they didn't say that, and believe it. But their view relates to the collective development of their entire body of professional talent. More importantly, it relates to the needs of their practice and their clients. What it doesn't necessarily relate to are your individual career goals, which only you can define.

Second, when you let yourself settle into the comfortable place of believing that someone else is handling this for you, you will very soon (and not unnaturally) stop thinking about it. As a result, you will stop passing career development decisions through the all-important screen that asks, "Is it right for me?" I've personally seen this happen a number of times. Many of those situations ended badly when the individual one day realized that his career development had not brought him to where he thought he would be, or perhaps had stopped altogether several years back. Perhaps this realization occurred when the individual was counseled out by the firm as it sought to reduce salary costs–a process that focuses immediate attention on those employees whose future is seen to be limited. That's a harsh time to realize you haven't continued to grow professionally as you fully intended to do at the beginning of your career.

Third, you seek to be a professional, which means thinking objectively and independently about what you observe around you. If you truly want to be a professional person, you must make your own decisions about your responsibilities to yourself.

By taking decisive command, what I want you to do most of all is to continually ask yourself, *"Where do I want to go with my career, and what do I need to do now in order to get there?"* I absolutely guarantee you that after a few rounds of this, you will begin to come up with different ideas than your advisers within your firm.

This is not to say that your interests will necessarily run counter to theirs. Not at all. In fact, I believe this practice is also in the best interests of your employer. My experience tells me that most of the individuals in a position to advise you are actually very uncomfortable being placed in the position of responsible party for your career. You can help them do a better job of advising you on your career development if you bring your own ideas, needs, objectives, and critical thinking to the table.

Look at it this way, when you think critically about the present and future needs out there in the marketplace and how you can build skills to serve those needs, don't you think your employer benefits? You bet it does, and the smarter ones know that. That's called entrepreneurship, a highly valued commodity in today's economy. That's also how professional firms grow and thrive.

But what if all of this looking and thinking leads you to the conclusion that your present firm is not the place for you to build the career you're looking for? We'll take a look at that a bit later in Chapter 16. But first, let's take a look at three objectives that you should adopt that will add markedly to your career development. They are aggressively building knowledge, seeking the right experience mix, and managing others.

Aggressive Knowledge Building

If cash flow is king to your firm, knowledge is king to you. In today's economy, there's simply no substitute for a large and diverse base of knowledge. This was also true when I began my professional career in the 1970s, except that the characteristics of this knowledge base are remarkably different today than they were then. Let's look at these differences, and you will quickly see the trend.

Traditionally, once one had access to it, a professional base of knowledge was a relatively easy thing to acquire and manage. It was hard work and required intelligence, but it was easy to know where to go to get it, and what one had to do to maintain and enhance it. Professional knowledge didn't change much. This was generally true whether that knowledge base was the income tax code and regulations (as it was for me), the characteristics of construction materials, or even the theory and practice of organizing and managing a corporation. In a way, I suppose, the limitations of the human mind and its ability to absorb and retain new information had placed a practical boundary around these knowledge areas and contained their growth, permitting them to expand only at a certain, humanly manageable rate.

Then came the technology revolution. The exponential development of the power of the computer blasted through these boundaries and allowed a huge pent-up demand for information and knowledge development to run free. My own professional interest, federal tax law, was one of the first to experience this, thanks to the legislative process. The huge pent up demand in this case was the (highly suspect) need for Congress to build more complexity into our tax structure in never-ending attempts to manage our communal behavior, and generate revenue to fund our also-expanding government. As it began to dawn on our elected representatives that computers could be programmed to easily, and in mass, deliver income tax returns containing highly complex calculations, they began to build in more and more of this complexity. Deductions were phased out as income levels increased, interdependent calculations were required for the taxation of Social Security payments (that as a result defy understanding by the vast majority of the people who have to make them), and real estate transactions came to require at least three different taxation schemes, just to cite three examples.

The year that I began my professional career, the Internal Revenue Code was contained in one paperback volume of around 300 pages, and the companion regulations took up two slightly smaller volumes. Today, the paperback versions of these two sources would easily be three to four times as large. And the pace of this growth is still accelerating. Between 1954 and 1969, the tax code was almost untouched by Congress. Then from 1969 to 1984 (also a 15 year period) it was amended almost annually with major new schemes that required a great deal of study for consultants and hoards of Internal Revenue Service lawyers to interpret through companion regulations, some of which are still unwritten. For the practitioners of my generation, staying up with these changes became more time consuming than the acquisition of the original knowledge (which, by the way, has now been largely superceded).

And while this was happening in Congress, similar changes were also occurring in our clients' businesses and within other taxing authorities that had jurisdiction over them. It quickly became apparent that our old assumptions about how our clients did business, and therefore how they were taxed, could no longer be relied upon. All manufacturers, for example, were no longer created equal in the way they were taxed. If one client sold its products offshore, it might be subject to a taxing scheme not available to its next door neighbor whose only foreign sales were to, say, Nebraska. Yet we also had to know about an equally complex tax structure in Nebraska, because that state might have a claim on our client for tax on its sales there, but only if the company had a salesman who stayed overnight in that state more than two times per year (or some such). You get the idea. Thus, we had to know ever more about our individual clients and how they operated their businesses in order to insure they were getting complete and competent tax advice. We had to become knowledgeable in two ballooning specialty areas, the tax law and the business operations of each client we served.

Each profession considered in this book has its own version of this story. The point is the need to continually keep your knowledge current. As my own experience demonstrates it is no longer enough to simply acquire a base of knowledge in a particular area.

Adding value in any professional community will increasingly require that you build a second, and perhaps even a third, knowledge base that you can draw upon, in combination with the first, to service your clients. This is truly an area where 1 + 1 can easily equal 3, and where 1 + 1 + 1 might equal 7 or 13 or some even greater value. This will be the payoff in the future with the ever more specialized business community where we find and service our clients.

Find a second specialty to put with your first. And don't wait to start until you've mastered the first. You'll never get there. This second specialty could be another profession. A longtime friend was a nurse. Then she went to law school and became an attorney, thereby tripling, virtually overnight, her value in the marketplace as an attorney specializing in medical cost recovery cases. Another option in today's increasingly open markets is to build a base of knowledge in a particular geographic region of the world, perhaps to complement a fledgling foreign language skill picked up in the classroom.

Seeking the Right Experience Mix

If your knowledge base provides the vehicle for your career, then the right experience mix provides the fuel. This represents the propulsion material to put your knowledge base where it can be of the most value. And this element is often much more difficult to come by than the knowledge itself.

Your firm is certainly your best and probably your only resource for this experience early in your career. Persuading your partners to give it to you is made notably easier if you are known to be taking charge of your own career, and if you are viewed as a performer. There is no substitute for this performance element. If you set yourself up as a valuable resource, as someone who can help the firm achieve its own goals, as someone in charge, then your firm will bend over backward to make the right experiences available to you if it can.

So, what are the right experiences? They are experiences that let you answer yes to several questions. Let's look at these questions individually.

First, *"Will I grow through this experience?"* You want to be challenged professionally. This means using your existing knowledge base to work in situations that are different from others you've been exposed to in the past. And through these experiences, to not only build application skills, but also expand your understanding by using your knowledge in a different way or a different context.

Your firm will want to give you this multidimensional experience. You'll be more valuable to it as a result. But you'll have competition. To quote one of my favorite lines from the movie "As Good as It Gets," *"Everyone wants that!"* If you are viewed as a performer, you'll be equipped to successfully compete with your contemporaries for those prime assignments.

Recognize, though, that your firm also has a built-in bias toward having you repeat the same experiences over and over again. As you gain experience with a particular task, you naturally become better and faster at it. This will make you more efficient, and for the same client fee, your firm will be making more money. You have to go along with this to an extent. It's the way that you repay the firm for all the great experiences you're having. So, as a part of your answer to the first question, you might ask yourself with respect to each assignment, *"On balance, with this project will I build new or apply existing knowledge?"* When you find the balance on successive projects continually weighing in on the application side, it's time for a conversation. And it's not always easy to find the right point to say to the partners, "I've done this enough. Now how about a different assignment." This takes judgment and political savvy. I'll have more to say about those things later.

So the balance question relates to the diversity of the experiences you're getting with the same knowledge base. The next question goes to the other extreme. You should also be asking yourself, *"Is this the area where I want to focus my career?"* If a particular assignment is within the area you've chosen, then it's a really good idea to test your earlier picture of what you wanted. At the beginning stages of your career, your knowledge of your chosen area is incomplete and immature. It's not at all uncommon for professionals to change their intended focus several times in the early stages of their careers.

Inevitably, however, you will also be given assignments that stretch the boundaries of that technical area, or perhaps even fall completely outside of them. As you become known as a performer, your superiors will think of you as a problem solver and you'll be given assignments that require creativity, skill, and self-confidence. These will not always lie within your chosen area, but they will provide you an opportunity to change the boundaries of your focus and see how a new area relates. Ask yourself, *"Should my focus include this area? How does this area relate to mine, and are there natural relationships between them? Should I consider abandoning or postponing my commitment to my chosen area and look at this one?"* In my own experience, more really noteworthy professional careers have found their focus through the luck of the draw than through solitary reflection. Keep your eyes open and your antennae up. Be opportunistic.

The final question relates to those with whom, and particularly for whom, you work. Ask, *"Whom else in the firm should I be seeking to work with in order to expand my capabili-*

ties?" Working with different bosses, whether they are partners or simply more senior staff people, is a skill builder.

---

*I was surprised as a young staff accountant that
two managers, both longtime firm employees who
received virtually all of their training in the firm, did
things so differently and, by the way, each demanded that I do things his way. Not things where the
procedures were required by firm policy—those they
did the same. It was the small things. Usually, neither technique was inherently more efficient or
effective. Yet in working with each of them, I very
quickly decided which I considered the more efficient and effective for me.*

This, of course, is how different systems proliferate
within the same organization. You make your own observations. Other people make theirs. But the opportunity to
have these different experiences is a critically important
building block for most professionals.

Managing Others

Your value to your firm, and in the professional community in general, is greatly enhanced as you develop the ability to manage larger and larger projects employing greater
and greater numbers of other professionals. Managing others, however, is not always easy and doesn't come naturally to many people. This is especially true in the professional community for at least two important reasons. First,

the pressures of the project calendar often bring out the worst in people. Normally rational and likeable folks become time bombs with shorter and shorter fuses as the clock runs down. Managing others to achieve performance excellence requires, among other things, sensitive and thoughtful human interrelationships. Many would-be managers simply cannot find these qualities within themselves when the pressure is on.

Second, to make matters worse, professionals don't always come with all of the right gear to be effective managers. The professions are essentially technical disciplines. The perception persists that if I'm smart enough, and accumulate the right technical knowledge, and apply it in a number of situations, then I will be successful. There's very little touchy-feely stuff in that last statement. In other words, many professional people develop the impression that getting along with, and particularly managing, other professionals is not a part of the deal. That's a mistake, and a very unfortunate one at that. The good news is that each of us comes with a basic understanding of what it is to be human, and that's a pretty good base upon which to build the people skills required to manage others.

In watching others (and sometimes myself as well) manage within the professional world, it has often struck me that good managers delegate responsibilities, while not-so-good managers abdicate them. Abdication means to me that a project or responsibility is simply dropped on the desk of a subordinate, whereupon the abdicator washes his hands of the whole thing. Delegation, by contrast, involves several preliminary and follow-up steps that amount to the supervisor remaining engaged with the subordinate until the project is brought to a successful conclusion. Abdication often seems motivated by a desire to get rid of a problem, whereas delegation involves a desire to complete a project efficiently while at the same time enriching the skills and experience of a subordinate.

But (you ask), isn't the idea to let the subordinate take the responsibility and determine her own way to successfully complete the project? While that idea is not wrong, it's not complete either. The abdicator usually gives little thought to such things as the best way to approach the project, whether the subordinate possesses the skills needed for each phase of the work, how the project fits with the subordinate's other responsibilities, and how the supervisor's involvement might add to the educational value of the project for the subordinate. Expectations for timeline and budget are often unrealistic, if they exist at all. Effective delegation considers these elements and more, particularly when the subordinate lacks experience.

Abdication involves a sink-or-swim experience and supports survival-of-the-fittest personnel development (that is, so long as the abdicator gives the subordinate credit when the project is successful, which doesn't always happen). At best, it might give a truly outstanding subordinate the opportunity to take up a very difficult challenge and shine. Delegation, on the other hand, supports the growth and development of a much wider array of capabilities and people, and therefore the organization as a whole. It's also a better way to get projects completed on time and on budget. In short, effective delegation increases leverage while abdication inhibits it by simply handing off a responsibility from one individual to another.

I recall hearing a Navy admiral define leadership once as 1) understanding the situation, 2) knowing what to do, and 3) marshalling all available resources to get it done. That's not a bad definition of management either. Good managers have a clear and explicit vision of the client need being addressed. With this in mind, they take the time to apply their experience and skills to map out the specific steps to reach a satisfactory solution. When this involves a large project and team, they come to an understanding of each component part and what must be accomplished within it. This understanding is complete enough that they can specifically articulate it to others and thereby provide the general roadmap for each subordinate.

Delegation, then, is the part about marshalling resources. Not only is the delegator's vision complete enough to get the subordinate started, but it also permits the manager to assist the subordinate with efficient and non-intrusive support along the way–and to do this with several subordinates at the same time. Abdicators, by contrast, tend to be people who don't think a project through in advance but simply figure it out for themselves as they go along. Consequently, they are handicapped in their ability to plan a project with a subordinate and then come back into it as needed to help deal with the rough spots. They don't relate to the subordinate's processes because the only way they can see to do the project is their own.

As firms and projects grow larger, and as client demands for reducing professional fee levels grows more intense, the need to work in teams, and to have those teams competently managed, will only grow as well. The ability to manage other professionals needs to be a part of your tool kit. You need to welcome, and to seek out opportunities to gain competence in managing others. But you need to do two other things along the way.

- First, pay very close attention to the managers you work for. Watch the ways they interact with you and your team members, and ask yourself questions like, "What things does she do that motivate me and the others to perform better?" "What things produce the opposite result?" "How does this person help me to be more effective?" "What things do I see this person doing that I admire?" Keeping a journal is an excellent way of memorializing these observations for use when you are responsible for the performance of a team, and especially for the professional development of its members.

- Second, find ways to help yourself grow as a manager. There exists in the marketplace an overwhelming volume of material on management–books, workshops, tapes and video programs. The difficulty is in sorting through the options to find a manageable source of good material for yourself. One source is the American Management Association, a professional association dedicated to developing management competence in business. In its catalogs, you will find an amazing variety of material to help you understand the management challenge and develop your own ideas of and knowledge about effective management principles and techniques. Your own professional association may offer additional choices.

Seek out materials and courses that focus on managing others within a service business context. Many of the classic management texts were written from lessons learned within the manufacturing environment, where individual initiative and creative thinking are less important (and sometimes even penalized) and where the career options are often very limited. Managing within the professional community, and particularly within large professional firms, is quite a different animal altogether.

Knowing Your Value

On the day that you first report for work with your new firm, your value in the marketplace has been pretty well established. You have probably gone through some process or other to interview prospective employers, and your new firm established your market value with the salary it offered. If you were fortunate enough to have received several offers of employment, you undoubtedly compared them and gave important weight to the levels of compensation being offered along with the different terms and conditions associated with each. As a result, you now have a pretty good idea of your worth as a professional. It will never be quite so easy again, but it will remain equally important.

You have a responsibility to yourself to maintain this understanding of your market value. In our free-enterprise system, it is a key component (some would say the key component) of your career progression.

In much the same way that you and your firm share a common need for you to grow as a professional, you also share a common need to understand your market value and assure that your compensation reflects that value. If you are undercompensated, the firm risks the loss of a key resource. If you are overcompensated, the firm will ultimately have difficulty billing a fair rate for your services. Either way poses a risk to the future of your relationship.

My experience tells me that far more compensation difficulties between a firm and an employee result from ignorance of the employee's value than from knowledge of it. There are many other critical elements in a successful employee-employer relationship, but employee dissatisfaction with any other element tends to manifest itself as dissatisfaction with compensation.

Numbers, particularly those that speak to one's value, are easy targets. However, it's a big mistake to view money as a cure-all. A raise will seldom, if ever, serve to compensate for bad assignments or for a perceived wrong or missed promotion. It will only serve to paper over the problem until it finds a means of exploding onto the scene in the future. Likewise, an employee who is undercompensated based on experience and capability will not be around forever, and will often, it seems, find a time to depart that is the absolutely least convenient for the firm.

It is far better for both parties to have a common understanding of the employee's market value, and to make certain that a corresponding salary level is established and maintained (or at least reconciled somehow). Recognize, however, that it is much easier for your firm to access this information than for you to do it.

Your firm, if it employs more than a handful of other professional staff, probably has several sources of market salary information. But you need your own independent sources. So what are some possibilities? First, periodically check the want ads. If your community has an active professional community, chances are the local newspaper want ads will reflect this. Do some comparison shopping. You'll probably recognize some competitors among the ads. In addition, a number of job-oriented websites can also provide the same type of information. Perhaps you and a fellow professional school graduate share a level of trust that permits you to discuss your compensation levels without reservation. Still another source is the search firms that specialize in your type and level of professional. Even if you are not interested in changing jobs, these firms can be a great source of market information. But recognize their bias in wanting you to agree to interview with another firm.

The point is that you should regularly update your knowledge of the monetary value of your services. This can be an important element, often the most important element, in a healthy trust-based relationship between employer and employee.

Performance Reviews

Virtually all major firms in all of the professions have some form of periodic review of each employee's performance. Expect it—and if you don't find it, demand it (tactfully, of course). At the very least, it provides you with an opportunity to compare your view of your performance with that of your firm.

This process has two distinct pieces, performance appraisals and performance reviews. A performance review is a more-or-less formal meeting between you and your manager or partner to discuss your performance over a specified period of time. This could be over the life of a project to which you have been assigned or it could relate to a calendar period such as a year. Your review might instead be assigned to a manager or partner with whom you've not worked in order to involve another person in your career development and help assure objectivity.

The content of this discussion with your manager is provided by performance appraisals, which are usually written documents in a standard format. These are completed beforehand by the supervisors to whom you've been assigned. If you've worked only under the direction of the manager who'll conduct the review, then all you'll hear about is his appraisal of your performance. If you've worked for others as well during this period, then the manager conducting the review will probably base his comments on an aggregation of the views of all of your supervisors as expressed in the performance appraisals they've completed.

Some firms start the year by working with each staff person to structure a personal development plan for the year. If your firm does this, it's a great opportunity for you to indicate the path you would like to follow and request the job assignments and education that will help you progress down it. Subsequent performance appraisals and reviews during the year will be benchmarked against this plan.

Performance appraisals and reviews serve several inter-related purposes. From the firm's standpoint, the process helps it to evaluate the skills and performance of each employee against its present and future operational needs. Thus, it helps to identify employees who are worthy of more responsibility and promotion as well as those who will likely not be able to contribute future value to the firm. Remember, the firm's employees are its machines of production. This is the process where the firm formally values the contribution of each of these "machines" in an effort to run a more efficient, profitable operation. This process also helps the firm identify any steps it needs to take in the future to help its employees be more productive. This might include such things as employee education, better management, or greater administrative support.

From your standpoint, performance reviews offer the opportunity to compare notes with your managers about your performance and get valuable input for your job of managing your career. This often includes guidance on how your skills relate to the firm's needs in all of its functional specialties. It might point your way to that new skill set that will complement the experience you've been accumulating. You might learn of a particular educational offering that you could take advantage of. The firm's view of your past performance and future potential, therefore, is highly valuable to your understanding of whether you're on track. Are you performing? And are you viewed as a performer?

Recognize going into this process that it is an imperfect one. In a very real sense, it focuses a tremendous amount of management attention onto a very small exercise. Emotions can be engaged, particularly those of the employee being reviewed. As a result, the outcome, be it negative or positive, can be exaggerated to an extreme. Great managers do such a good job here that even mediocre employees tend to come away feeling as though they've had an hour or two with the Super-Mentor-of-All-Time. And bad managers can botch the conversation so badly that even the best employees can come away wondering what they've heard and asking themselves if they have any future with the firm at all.

My experience, and many experiences of others that have been related to me, tell me that most firms do a somewhat inadequate job with the *process* of performance reviews, but generally end up getting the *message* right, even if it's sometimes difficult for the employee to figure out just what that message was. By this I mean that firms are generally pretty effective when it comes to evaluating how a particular employee is doing, what she needs in order to advance her career and become more valuable to the firm, and if she has a future with the firm. What firms don't do very consistently is paint a good picture of that for the employee, or at least for the average employee. The very strong performers usually see it, as do the employees who are not making it. But most of us, even if we have great futures with our firms, fall somewhere in between these two extremes. We just have to work a bit harder to extract the value that's there for us in the performance appraisal/review system.

Here's what you can do.

- **UNDERSTAND THE SYSTEM.** Ask: "How often are appraisals completed on me and my work? How frequently will I receive a performance review, and from whom? What does the appraisal form attempt to evaluate, and how is it scored?" These questions are often addressed in the employee handbook, but you should find out how the system really works. This is a good topic for a mentor.

- **INSIST ON REGULAR REVIEWS** (again, tactfully, of course). View this as a valuable employee benefit to which you're entitled. Help the firm stay on track here if you see it slipping. It's not unusual for deadlines to be pushed back, for example, for two appraisals to be combined into one, or for you to find that your October review isn't scheduled until after the holidays. Timing here is important. If the firm has a problem with your performance or if you might be able to attend an important education course the next month, you need to know that now while there's time to act on that information. Remember, as important as this process is (everyone will usually agree on this), it's not a popular thing to do—even for the managers.

- **EVALUATE YOUR OWN PERFORMANCE.** Go over the work you've done and score your performance against the firm's own criteria. And do this while it's still fresh in your mind. Even if your firm were not doing this, you'd want to. Remember, your career development is your responsibility. If you spot deficiencies, think through how you will deal with them and be prepared to offer your own plan. Highlight areas where, in your view, you were especially effective. Save up a list of these in case your supervisors haven't noted them. If you feel your performance entitles you to greater responsibility, identify what that might be. Some firms actually make employee input a formal part of the appraisal and review procedures.

- **PREPARE FOR YOUR REVIEW.** Go over your self-evaluations, including performance deficiencies and successes. And be objective. Your goal for the review should be for you and your manager to reach a consensus view of your performance and value to the firm. Be prepared to advance your own view of that. But beware, nothing will kill a manager's commitment to this process quicker than an overbearing employee who has an unreasonably positive view of himself and his performance.

■ STAY OBJECTIVE DURING THE REVIEW. This can be tough. If an element of your performance is being criticized, it's so easy to become defensive. I know. But focus on understanding the deficiency and learning from it. If the manager's comment is of a general nature ("You are doing this" or "You haven't been doing that"), ask for specifics. You can't change behavior unless you know exactly what that behavior is. The same goes for reinforcing positive behavior being observed. Remember, if your manager has elected to confront a negative issue in your performance (usually not a pleasant thing to do), far more often than not his motivation is to help you advance your career. And remember whose responsibility that is!

■ FORGET ABOUT COMPENSATION DURING THE REVIEW. Many firms have now separated performance reviews from salary reviews, and with good reason. While performance is a key element in determining compensation on an individual level, it is only one. Others include the profitability of the firm, the general availability of people in the market with comparable skills,

and the firm's backlog of work for you. These
factors can vary dramatically from period to
period, affecting the amount of adjustment to
your current compensation in the bargain.
While a raise this year is indeed very important,
focus your attention on the trend of your earnings and what that says about the progression of
your career.

If this process seems somewhat intimidating, then you'll
enjoy the fact that the partners in your firm probably have
to endure their own version of it. So take heart.

Your Firm's Value to You

An old saying where I grew up in Texas advises, "Dance
with the one that brung ya." It's all about loyalty of
course, and speaks to the ethic of respecting the relationship that brought you to the party. Your party is the profession that you are joining, and the one that "brung ya"
is that first employer. In this context, once you take a job,
you owe your new employer the total commitment of
your professional career as long as the partnership
between the two of you works for both parties. Your
employer is putting its energy into helping you succeed.
You are the partners' choice for the position you now hold
and you should expect that until and unless you prove
them wrong, they will continue to believe in you and
support your development.

For you, it means the job search is over, until enough
time has passed for you to know whether it's working. If
you do your part, it will be clear enough if it isn't. How?
Through your continual challenging of yourself—increas-

ing your experience and building your skills–and through the knowledge you gain regarding your value in the marketplace. If you find one of those indicators to be off course, candidly discuss your concern with the appropriate people in your firm. Until you have done that, I believe, you owe it to your employer not to be caught up in the possibilities that another firm or another industry might offer.

In addition to simply being the right thing to do, I believe this to be good business. As you build more and more relationships within the community, the respect that you gain among others will follow you. An individual who is continually looking for the next opportunity builds a reputation as a short-term thinker and opportunist. The negative connotation that those two terms conjure up when used in this way is not helpful in the professional community. They do not paint the picture of respect that is so necessary to a successful career.

Remaining loyal to your employer is not always easy in today's market-driven, information-intensive world. It is also complicated by the haste of some employers to lay off employees at the first sign of a dip in their business–the employer-side corollary to the short-term individual thinking noted above, which carries some of the same reputational consequences. I firmly believe, however, that you, the employee, will do more for your professional career by being loyal than by being a continual opportunist. Opportunists gain, in my view, only a temporary advantage at best. I encourage you to think seriously about this issue.

6

Managing Your Time

Effective time management may be the single most important skill a professional needs to develop, because time is
what professionals sell. A respected colleague of mine
believes that professionals sell expertise and price it by the
hour. I disagree, and I think the difference is worth understanding.

The most important commodity that any of us possess—our only real asset, one might argue—is time. And
time is a wasting asset; we deplete our supply over an

n period, our lives. How often have you heard someone say, "I just don't know where the time went"? To me, that seems terribly sad whenever I hear it spoken in earnest. I hope I'm not asking that question someday when the lights are about to go out on my life. I want to know where my time went, and to know that wherever that was, it represented a conscious decision on my part to invest it in living.

When I decide to dedicate a day of my life to a client, that's a day that will never again be available to me for any other use. It's been irretrievably spent. So I believe that as professionals we sell time, and we price the time we sell on the basis of the expertise that we possess individually and collectively as a firm.

One thing that makes this a difficult concept for many professionals (particularly young ones) is that one particular day, or even one particular hour, out of our relatively long lives is such a small thing as to amount to only pocket change, and who counts that? But is it? How do we really know on any given day how much undepleted time we have in reserve? And what is the worth of that day or hour? From our individual perspectives, how can we measure its value? The answer is, we can't.

Our clients, however, measure it constantly. They measure it in terms of the expertise we bring to their problems and projects. Our hourly or per diem rates reflect nothing more nor less than the market value of that expertise combined with the client's expectations about how effectively we can put it to work on his behalf.

The Challenge of Time Management

The art of time management is important to everyone, but as professionals, the need to master it is in front of us all the time. In a sense, we are fortunate to be reminded of this need in ways that those in other occupations are not. Selling our time by the hour, day, or project, we are continually faced with the practical aspects of time management in the form of time sheets and budgets, along with frequent demands on our time for non-billable tasks. We become very conscious of the need to manage this wasting commodity.

This unique circumstance demands that we take control of our days and assure that we are spending and investing them in ways that optimize our pursuit of our careers. Client service time is how we earn a living. That must get priority. But if we let client demands control us to the exclusion of all else (and this can easily happen), then we find one day that we haven't invested enough in ourselves. We haven't maintained the currency of our professional knowledge, or we haven't continued to build that knowledge. Alternatively, perhaps we haven't tended the personal side of our lives by spending time with family or by taking needed vacations. All of these priorities, and others, are important to our careers and our lives, and need their place in our days. Making all of those things happen and keeping balance in our lives is what time management is all about.

In Stephen Covey's book *The 7 Habits of Highly Effective People*, he distinguishes between those things that *demand* our attention (the "urgent" tasks) and those that are *truly important*. His point is that if we don't manage our way past the urgent demands on our time, then we are making a decision to let crisis manage our lives. The price we pay for allowing this to happen is never getting around to attending to the things that are simply important, but not urgent. These things, almost by definition, are the strategically significant things that will really make a difference in our futures and in our careers. These are things like keeping our professional knowledge current and building second knowledge bases that enhance our value to clients. And they can be unbelievably difficult to get around to among the excruciating demands of project deadlines and all of the other activities mandated by our clients and our firms.

A Few Suggestions

I've found time management to be a very personal thing. The techniques I use are unique to my own personality and style. My favorites won't necessarily work for you and neither will Stephen Covey's. Nevertheless, they represent a starting point as you build your own habits.

The most effective tool I use is a master "to do" list. I've kept one so long, and review it so regularly that I can usually remember the really important and urgent items on it. I include not only client projects and significant administrative tasks, but also important things that I need to get done for my own growth and career progress. I find a way to add any significant item that makes itself known in between the times when I review it (usually every two weeks or so). If I wake up in the middle of the night in a panic because of something I just remembered that I have to get done, I often get up and write myself a note. I add it to my list the next day if its midnight level of importance survives the cold light of dawn.

Periodically, I review the list in a very specific way to determine how I will spend my time over the ensuing several days. First, I place a checkmark next to every item that I *would like to get done* in the time period under consideration—usually a week or two. Note the wording "would like to get done"—it's very important.

Next, I go through the list again looking only at the items checked in the first round. This time, I place a second check next to those items that I *need to get done*. You see the pattern emerging. The final round involves a third check for those items that *have to get done* in the target period. This usually becomes my marching order for where I will focus my attention.

I have to be very careful in this exercise to consider both the items that are imposed on me by clients or others, and those items that I impose upon myself—the important things that Stephen Covey talks about. I'll let client demands usurp these items for a short period, but if I find that some very strategic things are not getting done, I screw up my resolve and give them a fourth check, which sends them to the absolute top of my task list. I have to say that when my system hasn't worked, the point of failure has been in not respecting this fourth checkmark. It's very easy to fight fires and let tomorrow take care of itself.

As well as this system has worked for me, the day-to-day implementation of it constitutes another, tougher battle. It's very helpful, even necessary, for me to start each week with a picture of what needs to get done that week. It's altogether another thing to make it happen as planned. Clients have new needs, projects stall for unanticipated reasons, "things take longer than they do" (to quote one of my favorite of Murphy's Laws), phone calls consume entire days–all of these things and hundreds of others work to derail my best intentions. So accomplishing all of my goals for a particular period sometimes takes what seems like superhuman effort. But where would I be if I didn't have a plan to begin with? No better off than a rudderless ship being blown around uncontrollably by the elements. Surprisingly, many times when I go back to my list at the end of a target period, I find that I've completed most of the high priority items (often all of them) and have made a significant dent in the second-tier tasks. So the system works for me; maybe it will for you also, until you find your own version.

Over the years, my biggest disruption has been administrivia, tasks that supposedly have to get done to keep the place working. This includes such things as time sheets, incoming mail, billing, filing, other record keeping, and simply keeping my desk clear of paper and other junk. This all sounds like necessary and beneficial stuff, I know, but I can become some-what compulsive about it. I've found that a very pro-ductive way to deal with this captivating diversion is to limit my administrative time to, say, one hour a day, and I commit a clearly specified hour to it. Then, I do nothing but take care of this stuff. If it doesn't get done today, I know that there'll be an hour available tomorrow to finish. This usually is a great help in allowing me to limit the time I spend on these rela-tively unimportant tasks and focus on the things that have the potential to really make a difference for me, my clients and my firm.

About Project Budgets

Project budgets vary considerably in their content and relevance among different professions, firms, and projects. They can be maintained on highly complex computer models that attempt to predict the critical path and time requirements involved in various contingencies, or be back-of-an-envelope numbers put together the night before a project begins. Often they are produced by the project manager, sometimes for his exclusive use in periodically assessing the project's progress. Ideally, the entire project team should be involved in developing the budget so that everyone is very aware of his individual role. Here's why that way is more productive.

However sophisticated the budget and its preparation may be and whatever its other uses, its principal value is as a communication tool. The budget is the principal means by which the project manager communicates his expectations about your role in the project. Typically, significant portions of a project that will be separately assigned to individual team members are budgeted separately. Therefore, you should have the opportunity to understand where your responsibilities lie and to discuss them with the project manager before work begins. This can be of great value to your perception of exactly what is expected of you, and allows you to gain an understanding of how your work will relate to the work of other team members. The project budget provides the framework for this understanding. Again, think communication and take every opportunity up front to understand the tasks that you'll be doing, how much time has been budgeted for them, and the results expected from you.

The budget's value to your firm lies in tracking the efficient completion of the project, and particularly in identifying unanticipated deviations. Communication is the key here as well. When the budget is prepared, it will be based upon certain assumptions. These will ideally relate to all of the important variables that may affect the progress of the project. For example, if the client is to complete certain preparatory work prior to your involvement, or is to actually complete a portion of the project alongside your firm's personnel, then the plan for your work will be based upon assumptions about the timeliness and competency of the client's efforts. If the client doesn't complete its work according to plan, then your firm may have to make up the difference or delay its work. This will likely increase project costs by necessitating increased staff time to cover the failure, or requiring the addition of personnel or supplemental skills. Other types of assumptions can fail for different reasons. When the whole team understands these assumptions and their impact on the budget, such deviations will be recognized quicker, allowing the manager to sort out their potential impact on budgeted time and, ultimately, the profitability of the project. If the failure is the client's, then the fee may be renegotiated to compensate, but this is much easier to accomplish if the team has not already made up for the failure with its own time.

As the project progresses, the budget will continue to serve as a communication tool. You should regularly compare your progress on each part assigned to you with the time budgeted for that part. When you detect, as you invariably will, that you are only, say, a quarter of the way through the work required for a particular part but have used half of your budgeted time to get there, you should immediately raise the issue with the project manager. You might be doing more work than is required, or the original budget may have been founded on an erroneous assumption about the amount of work involved. Or you might be doing work that adds more value to the outcome, in which case the partner may decide to renegotiate the fee with the client. In any case, it is far better to know this early than to piece it all together after you have completed the work and overrun the budget by 200%. Then, it's too late for anyone to take corrective action.

At the completion of the project, the budget (this time in comparison to the actual time it took for you to complete your part) serves as still another basis for communication. This time, it's the review of your performance on the project. Most firms now make this a standard post-completion step. If your firm doesn't do it as a matter of procedure, seek out your project manager for this conversation. This is an important learning opportunity for you. With the work still fresh in your mind, a review of your performance can help you visualize the strong parts of your participation as well as the parts that you'll want to focus on and improve. Successive post-completion project reviews can be an invaluable source of feedback on your career development. They also pave the way for increasing responsibility for you in future projects of the same type. Again, think communication and look forward to these conversations.

Finally, comparing the budget for a completed project with the actual performance of the team can be a valuable tool for budgeting other similar projects, or for budgeting the same project next time around if it is of a recurring nature. To get the most out of this use requires that a post-completion wrap up be documented with due regard for its future value and retained.

Why all of this attention to budgets? Because I have often found that project budgets are disrespected, particularly on smaller projects. They may be thrown together at the last minute without the involvement of those who will be expected to live by them. Or they might not be consulted for guidance during the project. Further, the project may be completed without anyone identifying the critical performance elements of the work, or relating them to the time taken to complete them. In short, they are often not used as the highly valuable communication tool they are. If you insist on benchmarking your performance on the budget and using it as the communication opportunity it represents, you will gain the respect of your project managers and gain significant professional development input in the bargain.

Playing "Heads-Up Ball"

Effective time management is a value proposition. Make sure you squeeze as much value as possible out of each unit of time you spend. You do this by getting assigned to projects and project managers that will challenge you and help you grow. And you do it by maximizing what you give to them. The quality of your performance is an extremely powerful time-management tool. The stronger your performance, the more effectively you've set yourself up to advance to the next level of learning. Through top-quality performance, you establish yourself as one to be reckoned with and build the ability to more effectively choose your projects and managers, thus advancing your career in the process.

One of the most effective ways to enhance your performance is by playing "heads-up ball." By this I mean being alert to all that you are exposed to in the course of your work, and using what you observe to add unexpected value to client engagements. For example, cross-selling the full range of its services is one of the most difficult things for a large and diverse professional firm to do. Cross-selling means getting clients who use one specialized function of the firm to agree to use additional services from another specialized function altogether.

Professionals tend to work with blinders on. The more technical the specialty, the more intense that person's attention on his own area tends to be. In order to effectively cross-sell, a professional needs to have his head up and in the larger game. This means being alert to the capabilities of his colleagues in other practice areas and also to the unsatisfied needs of the client. This requires some fundamental understanding of not just the skills of these individuals, but also the situations where these capabilities can be applied to benefit the client. In a firm that practices several different specialties, not a little effort is required to gain this level of knowledge.

A former client provides a good example. This large law firm specialized in work for an important local industry. Among the firm's strengths were highly competent attorney groups focusing on the laws regulating the industry, corporate mergers and acquisitions, tax law, and estate planning, to name the most prominent few. It also had a very large and successful litigation practice. Its trial lawyers were well-known in the community for the depth of their industry knowledge and their courtroom successes, and this group consistently represented a principal source of new business both within and without the firm.

It seemed an ideal recipe for success, yet the firm struggled to grow and ultimately failed. Its principal source of new clients, the trial lawyers, brought in a regular stream of just the right sorts of clients, but these clients usually became history after the litigation was concluded. In fact, the litigators were so focused on the demands of their own work that they seldom produced a connection between any of the clients they developed and the other specialties within the firm. They committed virtually no time to understanding the capabilities and successes of their partners, and gave only lip service to the need to cross-sell within their own firm.

To the firm's other lawyers, a particular client's need for litigation services was usually crystal clear. And their knowledge of what their trial specialists could do to help the client was equally well-grounded. Recognizing a referral opportunity in that direction was easy and happened

*often. But referrals in the other direction were
almost never made.*

Use some of your time to learn to recognize client needs
for other services that you don't personally provide, and
develop the ability to relate this to your colleagues in
other professional areas. I call this "connecting the dots."
Eventually, you should seek to build referral networks
across the full breadth of your business community to be
able to connect the dots with different types of professionals as well. More about this in the next chapter.

Another aspect of playing heads-up ball relates to the
project budget. A well prepared project budget will be
based upon certain expectations about the specific scope of
the work required. One of the real challenges in managing
a project is keeping track of these expectations so as to
avoid scope creep, or the tendency for the firm's work on a
project to grow larger without any corresponding increase
in the fee.

As noted above, project creep can result from the client
not fully completing its part of a project and the burden,
therefore, falling to your firm to complete it. In this case,
playing heads-up ball relates to being continually aware of
the work you're doing, comparing it with the work specified in the budget, and raising the flag when you discover
that you're doing something that is beyond the original
scope of the project. This allows the partner or project
leader to take this up with the client, thereby motivating
the client to complete its part of the work or, alternatively,
to pay more.

Occasionally, project creep will result simply from
your firm's recognition of a client need that was not

addressed in the project agreement. In this case, completing the work without its first being brought to the client's attention circumvents the potential client-relations benefit of your firm identifying and solving a problem that the client wasn't even aware of and eliminates the potential revenue your firm should reap from its initiative.

Time for Yourself

The final element of professional time, and often the most important and difficult to manage, is the time that we save back for the non-professional side of ourselves. In my research, I've found that this is consistently a source of difficulty among recent entrants into the professional world. It's understandable that this might be the case. Most new professionals such as you recently left the university campus, which is often a community unto itself. Your education, your social world, and many other dimensions of your life all took place within a very small community in a highly concentrated geographical area. In addition, you had a great deal of personal freedom on campus, and the time to structure your life as you chose.

Now you've entered a world where you no longer call the shots for the majority of your waking hours. Someone else is driving the train, and your time is no longer yours to manage in the ways that you've become accustomed to. Social relationships suffer from geographical separation, and because all of your friends now have their own careers to manage as well. Now that you've begun the career you have worked for for so long, you naturally want to devote as much of your time to it as possible. So your personal relationships and outside interests become the first casualties of your professional career. You can choose to live with this, or not.

Philosophers through the ages have universally told us about balance in our lives. Modern health science supports it. Your mother probably stressed it along with a balanced diet. They were all correct. A healthy life is balanced. An unbalanced life usually has to be corrected and shouldn't wait for a traumatic event like a divorce or heart attack. But these are mid-life problems, you say. They have no relevance to me at the beginning of my career. Well, maybe. But, on the other hand.....

One of the most important things you're doing at this point in your professional life is building habits. Many of the tasks you will perform, the routines you will observe, and the thought processes you will develop are new. Practicing them feels uncomfortable to you now, almost out of character. Sooner than you can imagine, though, this discomfort will disappear without you even realizing it. These things will have become habit and you will henceforth practice them without a thought, some for literally the rest of your professional career. So it is with your extra-career habits as well.

The point is that you owe it to yourself to build in a discipline of keeping a part of your new life for the things that make it all worthwhile, your family, friends, and wider interests. These things bring a texture to life that supports and enriches your professional performance, often more than you realize. You will perform better if you have somewhere else to go mentally on a regular basis, to uncork, and to get your head cleared and reori-

ented. If this includes regular exercise, so much the better for both health and career. And, as we'll see in the
next chapter, all work and no play not only makes Jack a
dull boy, but it doesn't help him expand his practice very
much either.

7

Relationships

The nature and quality of the relationships you develop, beginning in the early stages of your career, can be a factor in your success. For better or for worse, you are known to an extent by the company you keep. This is not an admonition to keep away from bad company, although I suppose that's important. Read it instead as encouragement to stay close to good company. I believe that when you focus on and carefully build positive relationships, avoiding the negative will pretty much take care of itself.

Good company, in this context, means company that can have a positive influence on your professional career. I am referring here to the full spectrum of ways to be a positive influence. I'm referring to your family and those others whose connection with your career is no more direct than that they simply motivate you to be the person you want to be. That, I believe, is an extremely valuable thing in itself. I'm also referring to the people who are closer to the center of your career—your colleagues, the people you deal with in your clients' organizations, your friends in the business community, and even your competitors. Let's look at some of these groups individually.

The Employees of Your Clients

This is a particularly important group when you stack it up against other groups you deal with regularly. Think about it—what group of people will have a clearer under-standing of you in a professional context than the people to whom you provide your professional services? What group will better know your professional capabilities and your skills in using them?

This group is important, therefore, for two reasons. They know you and they are already buyers of your services. If you do your part and perform as a professional, the people in this group are among those who can become your most ardent supporters and ambassadors in the community. And they multiply.

These people move about—they take new jobs elsewhere, get promoted—thereby opening up new opportunities for you. This represents a powerful multiplier effect working for you in the business community. A colleague of mine seems to be

perpetually receiving telephone calls from employees of former clients who remember him and his work and call when
they see a need for a service that he provides.

Your Colleagues

You see your colleagues on a regular basis. You work side
by side with them in the area where you will practice for
the duration of your career. These people pose a very real
opportunity for you, and I suppose a threat. They will
know your work better than anyone. Since they also specialize in what you do, they are in a position to develop
very strong impressions about the quality of your work
and the sincerity with which you serve your clients.

Like your clients' employees, these people also move on to
new careers outside of your profession. They might become
future clients if they think highly of your work. They may
become your future competitors who exploit the weakness-
es they've witnessed in your skills and character in ways that
can cause you real consternation. But if you've done your
part well, the professionalism that you've shown them as
you work together will be evident in the way they treat you,
whatever your future relationship may be.

In the Community

Here's a huge potential payoff area, and one to which you
should devote particular attention. It's so easy for a professional, with the tremendous demands of her profession, to
become very insular and focused on nothing but work and
career. When this happens, that person doesn't expand her
horizons in the broader world. By dedicating a part of your
life to involvement in some aspects of the community
beyond clients and professional work, you broaden yourself

and allow others to see your commitment to a better world.

This is where the true professional is recognized for what she is. This is where she becomes known as someone involved, someone who understands the fabric of her community and its needs. Her connection with others in this broader way truly brands her in the minds of others as someone worthy of their trust, and as someone who is a reliable source of solutions to needs in her professional area. Thus, the real connection between the professional and the broader community pays off for the professional in the form of a richer, fuller life, even as it puts that individual in front of the community as a source of needed professional services.

Good Citizenship

Within the world of professional services, and business in general, a body of largely unwritten rules of behavior can affect your relationships, and ultimately your career, in important ways. You may not even recognize that some of these rules are operating until you experience the frustration or insult of someone else not abiding by them. Let's take a look at some of them so that you can be alert to them in your own corporate behavior:

- BE ON TIME. Your time is valuable to you. As your career progresses it will become even more valuable in monetary terms. People who are not punctual compromise your ability to be efficient. Meetings that start late because the group had to wait on a delinquent participant effectively waste every member's time. Few things are quite so irritating as someone who is late to an appointment or meeting and arrives with a cavalier attitude about his lateness.

I once personally witnessed a firm (not mine) lose an important client because one of its partners was perpetually late for meetings and then was aloof and arrogant about it. There were undoubtedly other rough spots in that client relationship to begin with, but this partner's arrogance was what tipped it over the top.

Develop the habit early on of respecting the time of others. I know of no easier way to manifest this respect than to show up for your commitments on time.

■ DRESS APPROPRIATELY. This used to be an easy subject on which to provide guidelines. In recent years, it has become much more difficult as unwritten codes of attire have become more casual, and in some ways more important. Sometimes appropriate dress is more traditional. Sometimes traditional dress can be the kiss of death.

I showed up once for a meeting with an important advertising executive wearing a new and relatively stylish coat and tie that I thought would reflect just the right balance between professionalism and creativity. I was politely told in a hushed tone that if I expected to do any business with his firm, I would have to lose the tie. So I did.

The best rule here is to always be aware of the manner of dress of the people who are important to the particular circumstance, whether that be the client, the prospect, or the boss, and then customize it appropriately to yourself. If your client always wears expensive suits, then consider suits to be the dress code and wear a suit that's appropriate to your particular role in the relationship (i.e., probably not one that looks expensive).

I've found that people and groups that dress traditionally seem to be more dress-code sensitive. Therefore, I usually dress for the most formal person I'm meeting in a particular day, and reconcile myself to the fact that I may be overdressed in other situations that day. I've found that to be a good compromise most of the time. And if that's a suit, and my next meeting is with my advertising client, then I'll make up for the slight with performance, which is always the real test once you have the client.

One more thing–if all this fuss over dressing to please other people is a turn off, get over it. You have a chosen a life where other people's opinions matter to your future, and that's just the way it is.

■ PROJECT OPTIMISM. I suggest, just as a test, that you spend some time with the individual in the office who's continually down on something or someone. Soak up the environment that he creates. When you think you've got it, ask yourself how this person is influencing his career. Does he project the impression of someone who can be trusted? Of someone who can solve problems and find opportunities? Would you trust him to make important decisions on your behalf? Decision-makers responsible for buying professional services ask these questions every day. Don't think attitude doesn't matter. It does. And it reflects itself in the way we do our work. The power of the habit of positive thinking, I have come to believe, is one of the most important determinants of success in any endeavor, but particularly in the professional world.

- **AVOID OFFICE POLITICS.** Truthfully, I'm not even sure I can define "office politics," but the subject comes up as a negative in a surprising number of responses in my research. So I guess I'd better try. It seems to me that the term office politics usually relates to the phenomenon of attempting to advance one's career or gain some other advantage through personal interactions not directly related to performance. In other words, someone attempting to gain position on another by personally influencing a third person who holds a determining vote on whatever is at stake. Generalizing about this practice is tough. What constitutes unacceptable office politics to one person may look altogether like something else to another. I have been surprised many times by someone criticizing another for being political when all I observed was the other person just being polite and sociable. Having said that, I have clear recollections of a few people in my career who behaved unconscionably in their pursuit of the favors of a key boss or source of influence, and created real morale problems in the process.

In summary, whether you like it or not, what people think of you matters. In Chapter 8, we'll explore one of the key reasons for this.

Dating

Since the 1950s, employer rules prohibiting nepotism were thought to relate largely to the employment of spouses, particularly where one might be in a position of authority over the other. It always seemed to me that this situation could be very hard on the marriage, but it also offers the potential for favoritism in assignments, compensation, promotion, etc., which of course is why employers generally sought to ban it. The term nepotism, however, actually goes further. My Webster's Ninth New Collegiate Dictionary defines it as: "favoritism shown to a relative (as by giving an appointive job) on a basis of relationship." Until quite recently, employers sought, under the same rationale, to limit all extra-curricular relationships between their employees.

Today, for a variety of reasons, that has changed. But even though such prohibitions have largely disappeared, the basic problem they attempted to address has not. Romantic relationships with co-workers have the potential to be very disruptive of office efficiency. They can spawn time-consuming rumors, distracting in-office behavior, interpersonal jealousies and animosities, and sometimes outright loss of respect for one or both of the individuals.

This is not to say that dating a co-worker should be avoided at all costs. It is to say, however, that you should proceed cautiously if you do. Be aware of the potential for damaging your career and that of your friend if your relationship is not handled with discretion and sensitivity. You may have the best of intentions and still find yourself at the center of a controversy because of factors beyond your control, such as an office rumor monger or a jealous wannabe.

8

Marketing, Selling, and Expanding the Practice

In my research, I've found that many entry-level professionals express a high level of confidence in their understanding of their roles in growing their firms. In my own experience, however, I've found their understanding is often incomplete or simply wrong. The purpose of this chapter is to explore the subject that is often referred to as "practice development" and to establish a better basis upon which to build this important aspect of professional life into your career.

Probably the last thing you want to do in your professional life is to be seen as a used car salesman. Many young professionals feel this anxiety as they first encounter talk of things like selling the firm's services, cocktail party business, and client entertainment. While these aspects of practice development are real, the vast majority of professional services and projects aren't sold over martinis. More than that, selling them is fun. It's one of the true satisfactions in a professional career.

Why Do We Need More Clients?

One of the "Ah-ha!" moments in my career was when a mentor (and later partner) characterized our client base as a "wasting asset." That phrase captured a vision for me of an important phenomenon that is fundamental to many of the professions.

Some professions, and firms, live their lives off of one-off projects. A client becomes a client for one project and then goes away forever. The litigation section of the law firm I spoke of in Chapter 6 was a good example of this type and its limitations. Most professions, and most firms if they're smart about it, prefer to develop a base of clients with continuing needs so that one project is followed, within some reasonable time, by another. Auditing firms are a convenient illustration. Better yet is the client that uses a firm's services on a consistent and continuing basis. CPA firms, for example, provide large companies with continuing audit services. One of these engagements can last for years.

Any firm can become very comfortable in existing client relationships that yield year after year of "recurring, non-recurring" projects, to the point that their continuance is often assumed. After all, most clients would rather take a beating than switch major service providers. It can be a huge hassle, with many inefficiencies and hidden costs. So these relationships can continue for many years, sometimes indefinitely. And it's easy to fall into the comfortable conviction that they all will.

But the reality is that any number of things can end a client relationship in any profession. Companies are acquired by other companies that have their own professional relationships. Key personnel within a client company, or within the firm itself, can leave through transfer or retirement. Newcomers to these positions may have their own loyalties. And we're all human and can make mistakes that cause the client relationship to be reassessed. The point is, whatever your profession, clients regularly become non-clients and your client base shrinks. Thus, it is a "wasting asset."

If your firm's client base shrinks over time, and if your firm prefers (as most do) not to shrink with it, then lost clients must be replaced. And they must be replaced regularly to avoid the marketing inertia that would have to be overcome if marketing only began when the loss of an important client became known. But, even more importantly perhaps, most firms want to grow.

Growth is a naturally occurring need for any vital organism whether it be an individual or a professional firm. Growth enables a firm to expand its capabilities, and to add the depth needed to service growing clients. It enables a firm to earn the profits needed to pay competitive salaries and therefore attract new and greater talent.

It is a whole lot more fun to manage a growing firm than one that is stagnant or shrinking. When a professional firm contracts in size, all sorts of pressures build up for both employees and management around the need to reduce costs and produce more with existing resources. Growth, I would argue, is not an option for a professional services firm—it's a necessity. This need requires the consistent, ongoing effort that is known in most circles as practice development.

How Professionals Sell Their Services

Professional firms sell their services in any number of ways, but virtually all of them start with reputation. There are several components of professional reputation. Understanding these at this point in your career will enable you to begin to build this important foundation for your future. But first, a story.

When I completed graduate school and looked to the "real world," I was fortunate. Times were good, the economy was expanding, and entry-level jobs in my chosen profession were relatively plentiful. I had already left the campus mentally so I had no prob-

lem finding the time to interview. And interview I did. The very satisfactory result was a raft of offers to join the professional staffs of a number of very fine firms. As I later learned was typical, I quickly boiled my choices down to two firms, each very different from the other. The offer I accepted (after no little angst, I might add) was from the smaller of the two organizations. I felt that this firm was faster on its feet and more entrepreneurial, and that I could make a difference there that I couldn't make at the much larger firm. But it was really tough letting the offer from the larger firm go. This firm was truly the pillar of its profession. Its reputation was unsurpassed. It set a standard for ethical conduct that few firms could even hope to match. It was famous in the profession for its uncompromising positions, and added to that reputation regularly through stories of clients who chose to change auditors rather than bend to its will on a decision of propriety. These clients were always the losers in the court of public opinion, as this particular firm was such a pillar of virtue. The marketplace always assumed it was right.

That firm was Arthur Andersen, and it continued to live off of that fine hard-earned reputation throughout my entire career in public accounting. Then came Enron (and before that, by the way, a number of other failures that were not big enough to attract much public attention). In not much over six months from the initial disclosures of its flawed response to Enron's troubles, virtually all of its high-profile clients had deserted it, several of its large practice units had been sold off, and the firm and its partners were facing the very real prospect of bankruptcy. *Just imagine!* A near century old, worldwide, multibillion dollar professional firm, once the paragon of smart and ethical professionalism, was brought to its knees in the space of just six months. And all because of its reputation. When Arthur Andersen had it, its partners ruled the profession. Then they lost it, and they lost everything else along with it.

I know of no better way to make my point on the value of professional reputation and the consequences of tarnishing it. An extreme example? Without doubt. And yet to companies and individuals who value their own reputations, the standing of those with whom they do business will always be a threshold consideration. And for better or worse, your reputation as a professional extends into every corner of your life.

Professional reputation is not just about ethical behavior. It's also about being smart. It's about being technically competent, and about really helping people with real challenges, whether those challenges are solving an organizational problem or building a new headquarters building, designing a much needed information system, or structuring a complex legal agreement. It's about participating in the life of the community, whether that community is a city, an industry, or simply a network of business associates. And it's about being known.

The Marketing/Sales Process

Marketing the firm's services is a matter of attracting the attention of those who need them at the time when that need becomes recognized, and possessing the requisite professional credibility to be seen as the answer to that need. *Selling* the firm's services, on the other hand, involves persuading the prospective buyer to hire your firm over other, competing solutions available at the time. Together, they constitute the firm's practice-development process. The actual process rolls out in a variety of ways, depending on variables such as the type of service needed, the degree of technical sophistication required to perform it, and the availability of potential service providers.

While all selection decisions involve both personal and institutional considerations, the larger the project and the greater its complexity, the more the selection will tend to be an "institutional" choice between firms. Conversely, the smaller the project, all things being equal, the more often it will be a personal choice between individual practitioners. Large, complex projects usually require the manpower that only large firms possess. Likewise, large professional firms will ordinarily have greater technical depth and breadth than smaller ones. While the qualifications and characteristics of the individuals who will perform the work are an important consideration, they tend weigh less heavily if the selection is between institutional competitors.

Because smaller projects tend to be awarded to individuals rather than firms, these decisions tend to be personal. The decision-maker in the client organization simply likes the lead partner in one firm better than his counterpart in the competing firm, perhaps thinking that he will understand him better and be easier to work with.

Marketing the firm's services, therefore, begins with an understanding of where the firm is positioned in the marketplace, who its target clients should be, and the nature of the services that the potential client will require. Once these elements are understood, contacts, referral sources, and leads become the currency of the new-client development process.

More Practice Development Terminology

Contacts, in this context, are people in the community who know you and your professional capabilities, and who also know your firm and what it does. These are the people who can help you develop your firm's practice. They are your scouts in the field of battle. They may help by identifying prospects or prospective needs in your community, or they may simply be able to attest to your professional competence. Contacts are people you know. It doesn't much matter how you know them as long as they know what you do and have a personal loyalty to you and/or your firm. They need to be able to connect the dots in your favor when they hear of opportunities that your firm would want to know about.

One of my most unusual and valuable contacts over the years was a former employee whose employment I had been forced to terminate several years before. I was amazed that he thought enough of me to introduce my firm into a highly attractive new client opportunity. You never know!

Referral sources are those contacts who, usually because of their own business or profession, are in a position to refer work to your firm. Attorneys and CPAs are common referral sources for each other and also for other types of professionals. Both tend to serve multiple clients with needs for the services of the other. In this situation, attorneys and CPAs with a relationship of mutual confidence and respect can be important sources of business for each other. The same is often true with bankers, CPAs, and attorneys. In fact, it is not uncommon to see three-way relationships develop among professionals who are all serving similar types of clients. By definition, all referral sources are contacts, but not all contacts are referral sources.

Direct knowledge of a specific opportunity is called a *lead*. It can be a solid, or firm, lead where the source of the information is able and willing to introduce your firm into the opportunity. Or, it can be a soft lead where there is no direct path to take in order for you to gain an introduction into the situation. In this case, your firm's initiative and creativity will determine whether it will be able to attract the attention of the prospective client and secure an opportunity to submit a proposal.

A *Request for Proposal*, or *RFP*, is issued by a prospective buyer when the required services can be specifically defined in advance and the project specifications are complex. Governmental organizations often use RFPs to standardize the process of selecting a service provider and make it transparent. This is also a commonly used vehicle for soliciting proposals for complex architectural and engineering projects. In this case, the selling considerations are usually spelled out in the document, and little if any weight is given to personal considerations beyond the professional credentials and track records of the key project personnel.

Your Role in Building the Practice

So, how can you help? If you are committed to building a professional career, you already have a solid start with campus friendships that can aid your career development in the future. Your job now is to continue building friendships while those friends grow in their ability to help you, *and* while your professional capabilities grow at the same time. Let's face it, few if any of your friends will be influential enough to help for a while, and even if they were, your professional credentials do not yet include enough experience to justify it. Both take time to develop and mature.

You do this while you grow as a professional by talking about what you do. Share your experiences and milestones with your friends. Get excited about them. As you gain competence, you will also gain confidence in your ability to contribute to the solutions that clients seek. Your friends will see this and file it away in their impressions of you. At some point, when a need for what you do hits them in the eye, they'll jump at the chance to say, "My friend Mary can do that. Let me have her call you." That's when you'll know that you've arrived as a professional.

You'll want to give some serious thought to how you can expand your friendships within the business and professional communities. This will likely involve your joining groups that provide this opportunity. Civic groups are great for this, as are many types of charitable organizations. For openers, seek out a group with a focus that matches a strong interest of yours. This might be an amateur sports team or the support group for the local symphony or art museum. You'll have an easier time integrating into the group if you have a natural excitement for its focus.

Once a member, volunteer for projects. You can introduce yourself to members at meetings, but they'll remember you much longer after they've worked alongside you to help your organization. Real friendships are built here.

Later, I'll talk about your need to "build a life" for yourself amid all the stress of a professional career. Participating in a group that means something to you can serve two purposes—furthering your career and getting your head out of the office for a while. If you choose a group solely to meet its members, then it's still work. Find a good balance.

Understand that building friendships that can help your career is a long-term undertaking that takes work and discipline on your part. It takes a true love of your profession to pull it off. If you're not convinced that this is your life's work, you will convey that reservation to your friends. They'll know, believe me. They'll sympathize with your dilemma, and they won't hold it against you. But neither will they be getting the picture that you are a competent professional who can surely solve any problem that's put in front of you. You simply cannot create that very important impression without a true love of your work and commitment to it for the long haul.

Another place where solid relationships will pay off for you is with the members of your firm who practice in other specialty areas. Remember the law firm in Chapter 6?

Understanding the firm's other specialties and relating them to existing client relationships was the missing element among the litigation team and, if present, might have contributed significantly to the firm's survival. Cross-selling is a highly prized capability, and is usually very well rewarded by most professional firms.

9

The Role of a Mentor

A true mentoring relationship is a rare and wondrous thing. If you have just one such relationship in your career, count yourself very fortunate. It is rare because the attributes it requires are rarely found in concert among two people in the same firm at just the right time in their careers. And it is wondrous because it can greatly enrich the lives of both.

Being a truly effective mentor requires, first of all, taking a genuine personal interest in the career of person being mentored. It also requires that the mentor be in a position to observe that career and, at the same time, to understand what he sees. And finally, doing it right requires that the mentor have the skill and the self-discipline to provide truly effective guidance along with the willingness to commit the necessary time to the relationship. The required interest and willingness to commit are very personal things, the position requirement is pure chance, and few possess the skill to do it right.

As rare as ideal mentoring relationships may be, many successful careers are consistently attributed in part to the early influences of a mentor. This chapter is about who they are, what they do, how they influence careers, and why.

What Is A Mentor?

A mentor, in the professional context, is a wise and influential senior who takes an active interest in the career development of a junior, or protégé. In so doing, he often provides counsel, perhaps influences job assignments, and otherwise looks out for his charge's career development efforts. A wise mentor will leave his protégé alone to struggle, if struggling is the best way to learn, but will be there to help the learning process by aiding understanding.

A mentor, therefore, is a teacher who recognizes that life's lessons, particularly the tough ones, are often the best teachers. In that sense he is also a manager, doing what he can to assure that his protégé is exposed to the most beneficial challenges. And he is there to help assure that his charge learns her lessons, and translates those lessons into skills and habits that will result in the solid growth of her professional capability.

Successful mentoring, then, requires the wisdom and self discipline to be there only when the benefits of involvement outweigh the costs of helping too much. In mentoring, less is often more.

A true mentoring relationship works like family. It develops naturally, grows richer with time and shared experience, and leads to mutual respect, trust, and admiration that often transcends the business considerations upon which it is founded.

In the real world of professional services, the concept of mentoring has gotten a good deal of attention. Professional firms frequently have a problem with leadership. The knowledge and skills that make most professionals successful are technical and not necessarily people-oriented, and keeping up with a rapidly expanding knowledge base while serving a demanding collection of clients often leaves little time for the development of leadership skills.

One critical effect of this leadership deficit is often staff frustration that leads to high turn-over rates. Firms, particularly large ones that are unable to offer the high-touch environments of their smaller competitors, know this from performance reviews and exit interviews. In an effort to combat the negative bottom-line effects of this trend, many of them have attempted to institutionalize the mentoring concept. On balance, it seems to help, as indicated by my research on the first- and second-year experiences of professional staff people. But it usually falls far short of mentoring relationships that arise out of mutual affinity.

"Institutionalized Mentoring"

Surveys of recent professional school graduates tell me that many of the larger firms in all professions, and some of the smaller ones as well, have adopted the practice of assigning all entry-level staff a mentor. The role of this person varies from firm to firm, but it often begins at new employee indoctrination, involves what is essentially a career counseling agenda, and continues through the first year or two of employment. Most of the emphasis seems to be on the first three years of the protégé's career.

Most of these programs call for face-to-face meetings between the two parties at prescribed intervals. Some programs assign mentors within the operating unit to which the protégé is assigned, creating the possibility of a line relationship between the two parties. Others avoid this, perhaps for understandable reasons. Some afford the mentor a role in the performance review process if his protégé reports to someone else, but most also keep this function separate.

Some of these assignments develop into relationships with many of the classic mentor-protégé characteristics. Many survive one or another of the parties leaving the employ of the firm where it all started, or even the profession itself.

The world of professional services that most recent graduates encounter can be somewhat bewildering and discouraging, particularly after the honeymoon is over. Thus, new employees often genuinely appreciate interest shown by their assigned mentors. On a practical level, having someone to go to with questions about office routines, the expectations of managers, and often more personal needs such as finding an apartment or simply where to go for lunch, can greatly ease early anxieties and frustrations. And through the first year in particular, someone to help interpret performance reviews and even understand relationship issues with supervisors can become a real friend.

Making the Most of a Mentor Relationship

A mentor relationship is a partnership in a very real sense. Each party has a reasonably well-defined role, and both have responsibilities that are necessary for the effective outcomes sought by each. Let's look at these as a way of making the most of the relationship.

You will likely come to the mentor relationship hoping to gain insight into your career and how you can grow in professional capabilities and opportunities. You may hope that your mentor will be able to open doors for you when you're ready for greater challenges. You may see the opportunity to have someone on the inside to warn you of pitfalls along the way.

Your mentor comes with a very different set of wants. He likely sees an opportunity to help someone who is experiencing the same transitional issues that he experienced not too long ago, and will feel good about helping you. He may feel very acutely the effects of the high turnover the firm experiences, and be only too happy to do whatever he can to help reduce it. He may also see himself as a teacher and guide, and will get great satisfaction from doing that well. It's always possible that he's simply on an ego trip, anxious to have you see him as the source of all knowledge about the firm.

He is likely motivated by some combination of these. Remember, however, that his interests may not always align with yours. If your mentor is a supervisor in your own department, for example, his agenda to influence your job assignments may serve some purpose for him that's not necessarily good for you.

Early-Career Mentoring

Early in your career, your mentor will serve a very different function than may be the case later. At this stage, a mentor's principal function is to help you get off to a good start. In the first three years of so of your career, you will develop many of the habits and processes, both mental and physical, that you will use for the rest of your career. In the beginning, it's less about positioning you for partnership and more about helping you learn to ride without training wheels.

Here are three suggestions for things you can do to make the relationship work during this "apprenticeship" period:

- First, recognize that however it may fall short of your expectations, it is worth pursuing. Whatever the mix of your mentor's motivations, at some level each of them involves helping you be successful. So your first responsibility is to value the counsel your mentor provides and respect his desire to provide it. Nothing is quite as frustrating to a mentor as making his valuable time available to you and then seeing his counsel ignored without further discussion.

  This is not to say that you should accept everything he tells you as the only truth, or as something you should immediately do. As you know from Chapter 5, I firmly believe that you are the only person who can be in charge of your career. Every piece of advice and knowledge that your mentor gives you should be filtered through that screen of "Is it right for me?" But your mentor needs to know that you take him seriously enough to reflect on his advice, and perhaps bring it back for further discussion if you believe it doesn't fit. Differences of opinion are not fatal to the relationship if you handle them with sensitivity. However, if they are the rule rather than the exception, perhaps it's time for a change.

- Second, bring your issues to him. Seek him out. If he's in it to help you, as I believe is usually the case, he'll be pleased that you think enough of his counsel to seek it. To some extent at least, he's in this relationship for the satisfaction of helping. If you are never seeking his input, then you should ask yourself if continuing the relationship makes any sense.

- Third, be grateful for his interest in you. Even if an ulterior motive is part of what drives him here, the reality is that he probably has more to do than he can get done, and despite this he has committed to help you with your career. That's worth something, and you can thank him by being appreciative of his time and his wisdom. Your appreciation amounts to his compensation for his contribution to your career. Maintaining a sense of gratitude for his involvement will keep the relationship positive, and this is essential for you to see wisdom in what he tells you that is potentially beneficial.

- Finally, if you conclude after a reasonable period that this simply isn't working, consider discussing the situation with him. Develop a clear picture of the reason it's not working and what you need out of the relationship. Present this picture to him in an open and candid manner. But be sure to discuss issues and not personalities. If this discussion fails to pave the way to a more productive relationship, then see if you can work with him to have the mentor assignment changed. Remember, if he was assigned by the firm, this tells you that the firm has an interest in seeing it work. Ordinarily, the person responsible for these assignments will not object to a change, but will want to know the circumstances before doing so.

Mentoring For Professional Growth

Later in your career, a mentor relationship is a very different thing altogether. Here, mentors are not assigned, they are found. They tend to grow out of a mutual respect that comes from having worked together, probably on a regular basis for some time. They are often not recognized as mentoring relationships as a senior begins to take an increasing interest in the career development of his protégé. Usually, this relationship focuses on matters of greater significance and depth. This is where the line between mentor and friend is hard to find if it exists at all. Here, mentor is not a title, but a loose informal relationship.

Not everyone is lucky enough to have a true mentoring relationship such as this. Often mentoring relationships at this stage in the career of the protégé do not develop this depth. Some don't develop at all. The characteristics that seem to spawn these very special relationships are as varied as the people involved, but usually involve personal chemistry and mutual admiration. Mutual respect is key, and is highly dependent upon the performance of the junior. The senior's interest in the junior usually starts here. He is seen as a "comer" who can potentially contribute great value to the firm. And then the impulse to guide and to help grows in the senior and a mentoring relationship begins.

It should go without saying that the more influential the mentor, the greater the relationship's potential value to the protégé. And this more influential mentor will generally take an interest in the careers of the juniors whom he believes to be the most promising. Thus, your performance will, more than other factors, influence the development of a mentor relationship that can be of the greatest value to your career development.

Take a lesson from this. A career counselor may help you get a stalled career back on track, but a mentor will be there to help the individuals who are already very much on track. Performance here is essential.

10

Business Travel, Etc.

You will almost certainly encounter elements of professional life that are new to you; travel may be one of them. If a parent or close family friend was in the professional world when you lived at home, you already know something about work-related travel and socializing. If not, what you'll encounter might just as well be the cultural norms of a foreign country.

Some Background

Very soon, you will likely find yourself scheduled for a business trip. This may be in connection with a client project, a firm meeting, or simply a continuing education opportunity. Often you'll be traveling with others from your firm. A few general rules might help you be comfortable with this experience.

Many firms, particularly large ones, have very specific procedures governing employee travel. This often results in large part from a need to control travel costs. Think about it for a moment and you'll understand why. Parking you for a week in, say, Chicago or San Francisco can cost several thousand dollars. Airfare alone will likely cost several hundred. Hotel accommodations usually run well over one hundred dollars per night. And meals, particularly at urban business district restaurants, will add another hundred or so per day. Then there's local transportation, tips, and an array of incidentals. It adds up very quickly.

An airline ticket purchased close to the departure date can cost many times what the same reservation would cost a few weeks in advance. Hotels often offer the same sort of savings for advance reservations. For this reason, your firm will want to plan your business travel for months or at least weeks ahead. One person (or perhaps an entire department if your firm is large enough) may be responsible for purchasing travel and lodging for all of the firm's personnel. If your firm works this way, the bad news is that you're sort of at its mercy for the arrangements, but the good news is that you won't have to spend your valuable time making them or answering for their cost. If you are left to make your own arrangements, then be sure to ask your manager or mentor for guidelines and suggestions, particularly as to appropriate spending guidelines. Your firm's culture will dictate what is and isn't appropriate.

Bear in mind also that your firm's sensitivity to travel costs will almost certainly vary depending on its current backlog of work and its profitability. In good times, your partners may talk a lot about the high cost of travel, but the reality is that getting the work done will be of primary importance. Almost whatever has to be done to accomplish this will be viewed as a cost of doing business. In tough times, though, one of the first targets of the inevitable cost cutting mania will be travel budgets. If layoffs are happening in your firm, it's not a good time for you to be living it up on the road.

Ordinarily, your out-of-pocket costs for business travel will be reported to your firm on an expense report, which will be its basis for reimbursing you. This routine may be subject to a per-diem guideline for how much the firm will reimburse you for recurring daily costs like meals, laundry, and phone calls home. Alternatively, you may find that your firm simply reimburses you a fixed amount per day away from home to cover these things without regard to what you actually spend. This saves everyone the hassle of saving receipts and accounting for relatively minor amounts. It also saves money, as the firm establishes this limit and can enforce it much more easily than by questioning the appropriateness of what you've already spent. In my experience, most firms are reasonably generous with per diem allowances, and they don't really penalize anyone involved.

Procedures for expense reimbursement vary from firm to firm, so you'll want to find out how this works before you leave. Many firms will also provide you with a cash advance to cover out-of-pocket costs if they are expected to be significant. Chances are, however, that if the firm is purchasing your airfare and accommodations directly, you'll be expected to finance everything else and then seek reimbursement.

Life On the Road

The culture of business travel can be amazingly varied between firms, engagements, and even among the individual managers that you may work for when traveling. A roll-with-the punches attitude will be extremely helpful in dealing with the wide range of circumstances you'll encounter. Just getting there and getting back can often be a real hassle as a result of airline delays and cancellations, time spent waiting for ground transportation, and botched hotel arrangements. These experiences are usually the exception, but you'll need to be emotionally prepared for them. If you travel enough, they'll happen to you sooner or later.

The conditions under which your project is scheduled and managed will also vary. There's often an after-hours mentality of, "since we can't go home, we might as well work." If the project is on a short time deadline or if your manager needs to get home for an anniversary, you can count on lots of pressure to put in extra-long days. I usually liked this as it meant that I too would get home sooner. Carried to an extreme however, it can become pretty unbearable in short order.

When you do knock off for the day, you'll likely do some off-the-job socializing. Project teams on the road tend to hang together at the end of the day. This usually involves dinner and perhaps an after-dinner trip to a local pub or other hangout. Up to a point, this is part of the job, and you owe it to yourself to take advantage of the opportunity to get to know your colleagues on a personal level. The later the evening becomes, however, the more comfortable you should feel about bowing out for some time to yourself. If the team norm involves everyone hanging together until the wee hours of the morning and that's not what you do, then be a leader and break the norm. It's not a good idea anyway–for several reasons.

When you're dining out with your team in a large, expensive metropolitan area like New York or Boston, it's easy to watch the cash register ring up really large numbers in a hurry. This is often OK, or at least tolerated. It can be a way for your firm to ease the personal stress of being out of town and working hard. Sometimes, an expensive meal is even considered a right of those in your situation. But if you don't have a per-diem allowance, just remember that there are only two choices for who ultimately pays the bill–your firm or your client–the two groups other than yourself who have the most to do with your career. So be careful.

The senior person in your dinner group can normally be expected to pick up the check. Watch that individual when ordering. If she's being extravagant, then order what appeals to you. If she's obviously watching the costs, then help her out and eat more modestly. Here's another situation where you should be sensitive and make sure you understand the norms at work.

When drinking arises, know yourself and then be yourself. I've traveled with groups that just had a beer to wash down a hamburger and then called it quits. And I've also traveled with groups that started with the beer, then had a drink followed by wine with dinner and then capped off the evening with liquor. You'll likely see a wide range of behaviors.

Being away from home and in a relatively closed society, it's easy to be influenced by others. Anticipate that this issue will come up and decide in advance what's right for you. I have often traveled with a group where one member chose not to drink at all. I can truthfully say that I never witnessed an abstainer being subjected to any pressure to conform, or suffering any negative outcome of not conforming. In fact, that person was usually respected for his commitment and often welcomed as a designated driver or city navigator.

The second drink-related rule is to never, never overindulge. You have absolutely nothing to gain, and a lot to lose in a business setting by losing control of yourself because of alcohol. You need to be known for your level-headed competence, and if this means passing up another glass of wine at the dinner table, then just remember why you're there. Your career is more important than a good time after work.

Other Work-Related Socializing

Work-related social gatherings aren't just for trips. Sometimes you'll be invited to parties to celebrate the conclusion of a major project or busy season, company picnics, and holiday parties. Many of these experiences will be similar to socializing with your team on an out-of-town assignment without the stress of being away from home.

These events serve very important purposes for your firm, and for you as well. For the firm, these gatherings help bring you and your colleagues together and promote camaraderie. The idea is that a staff that knows each other well will work more effectively together and represent the firm better in the community. Morale will be enhanced. So the firm invests in social events and hopes they will help define its culture in more human terms than might otherwise be the case. To some limited extent, therefore, your commitment to the firm will be defined by your participation.

Your opportunity is to use these occasions to build your network and learn more about your firm. Particularly in a large organization, this may be your only chance to get to know staff members assigned to other departments or projects. They also provide a vehicle to increase your knowledge of other types of clients and projects that you haven't yet been exposed to. This can be important information as you consider your own career development and the career alternatives that may be available to you within your firm.

Parties also give you the chance to get involved in planning and coordination. Being seen as a leader in office happenings will raise your profile in a way that may surprise you. Staff members, even at your experience level, will begin to view you as someone who is engaged and therefore knowledgeable in the workings of the firm. You'll be seen as someone who makes things happen. This perception of you can be of significant help as you begin to take on supervisory responsibilities. To the extent that you are already seen as a leader, you won't have to prove it later. It doesn't hurt either that your partners see you volunteering your time for something they view as important to the future success of the firm.

The personal guidelines you observe in travel situations generally apply here as well. There's no career value in being the life of the party, and attempting to do so may detract from your efforts to get to know the others with whom you work and to learn more about your firm.

Another consideration here is etiquette. While the Victorian Era has passed and eight-course sit-down dinners are seldom seen in the business world anymore, it's still a good idea to know what's expected of you. In these situations, it's amazing how regal a dinner group can become at just the sight of crystal goblets and candelabra. When this happens, you don't want to be the one who stands out as a social incompetent. Get a book and learn the basics.

While I've never read an etiquette book, I've usually been reasonably comfortable in these situations and always just assumed that anyone who'd been around the business world for a while was also. Therefore, I was hardly ever quite so surprised as when one of my partners leaned over to me at a formal dinner one night and quietly asked, "Which fork do I use?" I suspect he was never more surprised as well when he realized that his loud whisper just happened to land in the middle of one of those occasional moments of nervous silence that can suddenly appear out of nowhere. He was immediately surrounded by some thirty socially engaged dinner companions, all of whom were eager to answer his question.

II

Building a
Professional Life

Professionals do not simply exist in their offices; you'll be happy to know they have lives too. Often, the integration of career with life and vise versa can be a real challenge given the demands of your job. This chapter offers some tips on the important interrelationship of a professional's work with his personal life.

The Importance of Achieving Balance

I've always suspected that we are all hard wired with an internal guidance system that, if we take the time to listen carefully, will direct us to the life we are built to live. I also believe that as a result of our being created human, we were given choices. To me, quality of life is a function of how well we let our guidance systems influence the choices we make. This belief has a lot to do with my feelings on the subject of balance in life.

To me, balance means making real sure that I'm dealing with all of the directions that I get from within, and not just the ones that I like, or those that are most convenient at the moment. This little bit of independence has not always been easy to reconcile with my professional life, which has often demanded more of me than my guidance system liked. Make no mistake, I never had any serious doubt that I was being guided to pursue my professional career. But all the other parts of my life sometimes didn't get the attention they deserved.

Professional careers these days are almost universally demanding and jealous of other interests. The knowledge base required to support these careers and the demands of the clients we serve can usually be counted upon to take more from us over our working lives than such demands in other careers that we might have chosen. This is not all bad. We do what we do to be of service to others, and to gain the satisfaction that comes from being an expert.

But I believe that we also have to pay attention to the softer side of life, as our internal compasses encourage us to do. If we ignore that guidance, we often pay a stiff price, and often when we can least afford it. This direction is unique to each of us, but usually includes:

- real involvement with our families,

- a commitment to our communities,

- time for our spiritual natures,

- exercise for our bodies in parallel with our minds, and

- an engaging intellectual pursuit other than the books, computers, and challenges of the office.

These are the things, in balance with our lives' work, that make us human. These are the things, along with our professional dedication, that add richness and meaning to our lives.

Am I Human or Professional?

One of the mistakes I made early in my career was trying to always keep the different parts of my life separated. It somehow made sense to me that I could get more value out of the personal dimensions of my life if I isolated them from the professional side. That way, I reasoned, the professional demands on me somehow wouldn't infuse and dilute the time I committed to other things. I remember being anxious when a member of my church congregation learned that I was a CPA and approached me to do a small project for his company. I was concerned that I had somehow used the church as a forum for developing business.

The point I missed here was that keeping these parts of my life completely separate required a great deal of energy. It was hard work. I wouldn't allow the flow of easy transition from one part of my life to another. As a result, I missed the joy that professionals take in being professionals in all parts of their lives, and in interacting with friends and acquaintances on this basis. I was so worried about corrupting my non-work life that I missed important opportunities to enrich it. Fortunately, this little exercise was relatively short lived.

The lesson related above is not to suggest that it's OK to blatantly exploit any and all social interactions for business purposes. This would represent its own sort of imbalance and be as potentially harmful as my own experiment.

The value of interacting with the community as a professional was brought home to me later in my career. My firm assigned me to a support office in Washington, D.C., for a period in the middle part of my career as a partner. There, I served our other offices. My clients were inside the firm and all across the country, but I had neither clients nor prospects for my professional services in the local community. I found that I truly missed interacting with clients and with others whom I might help with my skills and experience. I missed being identified with my profession among those with whom I interacted on a day-to-day basis.

Social Relationships

Professional credentials mean something. They tell the world that you have successfully completed a course of study, and often an apprenticeship, and have a superior level of knowledge and skill in an area of great social importance.

Our communities value those who hold them. You are quickly accorded a higher level of respect once you become know as a professional person. People credit you with the perseverance to survive the system, and the dedication to serve the community.

But that's only the beginning. Being a professional person in a social world is really fun. The opportunity to interact with others as a professional is the opportunity to serve, to be a resource to others. Finding needs that you can help address with your professional skills is one of the really satisfying aspects of being a professional. Will people try to use cocktail party conversations to get free advice? Absolutely; but that's part of the game. That's your opportunity to answer one question, and then ask several of your own that tell the individual that you have the skills to look beyond their immediate need and see bigger issues that hadn't occurred to them. As your career develops, you will find more and more opportunities to serve your friends as clients.

I remember the first time that a close friend, someone I had known since high school, asked to become my client. I was elated. In one short conversation, he confirmed not only our friendship, but also his acceptance of my capabilities as a professional. The same individual later referred a business acquaintance to me, and the high was even greater. At that point, I knew that I had attained a new level in my professional career. I was now seen as both a friend and a professional. And it wouldn't have happened if I had still insisted on leaving my professional life at the office.

Community Involvement

Community involvement offers the same sort of possibilities, only on a much wider scale. Our communities still, on some level, expect professionals to give something back in exchange for the status they enjoy. How fortunate for us. This commitment of our time yields many of the same opportunities that were noted above, only in ways that are richer still.

I am consistently sought after for service on non-profit boards, for example. Because of my professional status, I am assumed to be capable of serving and committed to the community. I began serving on these boards very early in my career, and highly recommend it as a means of enriching your life. Within reason, this use of time exposes you to entire circles of acquaintances that you would not otherwise meet. Start early in your career, as I did, and you'll find that you begin to count among your friends an ever-widening circle of people. Eventually, you will start introducing people you know from different circles who don't know one another. Then, you begin to be seen as possessing still another valuable attribute, community connections. This can be of immense help as you build your circles of influence and, through them, expand your client base and your practice.

Your firm, if it's typical, will love this. Almost every professional firm strives to achieve recognition as a central part of its community, and of being committed to its health and vitality. It's important to the firm's ability to grow and thrive just as it is to you as an individual practitioner. Your community involvement helps the firm achieve this recognition. As a managing partner whose job it was to build my firm's image, I was continually looking for staff-level personnel who were interested in the well-being of our community and committed to improving it.

Helping your firm enhance its community profile is only one benefit of this commitment. The principal benefit will be for you as a person. Community service enriches your life. It gives you greater personal depth. The people you meet and with whom you associate expand your understanding of your community. You will find that you are able to relate to, and therefore support professionally, a wider range of people and needs. You will serve a broader population, and serve them better. And service to them will produce great personal satisfaction for you. After all, helping others with their needs is one of the principal reasons we're here doing what we do.

One word of caution: community service can be addictive. Many non-profit and other community organizations are quite resource-poor. That's where you come in. They exist only because responsible people help out with their time and financial support. These organizations always have needs, often very large needs. If you are a caring, concerned human being, it's very easy to get caught up in this and be diverted from your responsibilities to yourself and your firm.

You may remember a friend in college who became so involved in his fraternity that he forgot why he was there to begin with. The fraternity did great, his brothers loved his commitment, but his grades were terrible. This can happen with community service as well.

> *Not too many years back, I found myself serving on six non-profit boards of directors at the same time. I was always flattered to be asked to serve and, it would seem, always said "yes." Two met on the same night every month and another required a significant (and always growing) financial commitment. Just processing all the paper that was sent me was a challenge in itself.*

My best advice for early in your career–find one, or at most two, such organizations, do a really notable job for both, and see what happens in a couple of years.

12

Managing Your Wealth

You're not as rich as you think. I know it seems as if the salary you've just accepted is all the money in the world after living a pauper's life for the last few years. The level of your starting salary, if you're as fortunate as many recent professional school graduates, is indeed generous and should let you set a comfortable living standard by most campus comparisons. But before you commit to a large rent payment, buy an expensive car, live it up on your credit card, and otherwise mortgage your future, let's consider a few things.

Through numerous conversations and surveys, I've learned that a surprising number of professionals in the first few years of their careers develop financial habits that lead to frustration. This tendency seems particularly acute within those professions that are not money-oriented by nature. We'll look at a few of the number of negative consequences of this tendency in this chapter. The good news is that they can virtually all be avoided by developing good money management habits early in the game. We'll look at a few of those as well.

Why Good Money Management is Important

You have two important career responsibilities to yourself–maximize the value of the opportunities that are available to you, and invest in your professional future. It's easy to see this in practice when you reflect on how you spend the hours that you dedicate to your profession. If you spend all of your available hours serving clients and none in building your bench strength as a professional, you will someday find yourself dated and irrelevant.

Managing finances takes planning too. As in managing your time, the secret to managing your money is very simply to determine the mix that's best for you before opening your checkbook. But in doing this, you've only crossed the threshold. The rest of this battle is won with self-discipline, a resource that's not always easy to muster up when you need it. But you don't get to fight that battle at all without first doing the planning.

Good Money Management Starts At Home

So the first question is, how much of your earnings will you permit yourself to spend and how much will you invest to accomplish your longer term goals. First let's look at the *mandatory spending* that you will need to consider. You must of course have a place to live, and unless you're well out of the ordinary among your contemporaries, you'll need transportation of some sort. A basic business wardrobe will be required, although its composition will depend on your firm, profession, and geographic region. You need to eat and to regularly buy all the stuff you need to function, like toothpaste and deodorant. And don't forget utilities.

Mostly, you don't have a choice about whether or not to buy these things. You do have a choice, though, about how much you spend on them.

Many other mandatory expenditures are easy to overlook. Taxes will take a big chunk out of a seemingly large paycheck. Cars require insurance, regular (and sometimes not so regular) maintenance, and, in some states, big property tax payments. Student loans must be repaid. Medical services cost money whether through doctor and hospital bills or medical insurance premiums, unless you're fortunate enough to work for one of the very few employers that still shoulder this entire load for you. Church or community contributions are often in this category—considered necessary but often forgotten until an inconvenient time.

With a few notable exceptions, these items may not be all that significant when considered individually. But when added together, they can amount to real money. By the time you provide for these basic costs of living and working, even if your individual purchases are frugal, you very likely will not have as much income available for *discretionary spending* and *investing* as you thought.

Let's see how much that is. Start with the amount of

your monthly salary and deduct your best estimate of what your mandatory monthly spending will need to be. For now, consider only the *minimum* level of expenditure that you can get by with. If you have an older car that you can get another year or two out of, base your estimate on what it will cost to simply keep that one rolling, rather than buying the new one you've counted on for the last few years. Assume, just for the next few minutes, that you share an apartment, or that you'll rent an efficiency—only the basics. Base your food estimate on all meals at home—no restaurant dining for now. In the case of expenditures that are typically paid less frequently than month-ly, just estimate a monthly equivalent.

When you complete this computation and deduct the results from your monthly pay, the remainder will be your discretionary income, the funds you'll likely have available for more satisfying uses. This is what you will spend on the fun and the comforts you want, *and* it will be the source of funding for your investments in your future.

The Icing on the Cake

I suggest at this point that you spend some time reflecting on the picture that you've just painted of the lifestyle you'd live with only minimum expenditures on the basics. Consider the things that you will really want to change. What luxuries (truly they are luxuries because they exceed what you really need) will you want to add? The answer to this question will determine how you spend your discretionary income.

Think it over for several days. Your feelings about some of these things will change from day to day. And remember this! *You will likely never have another chance, in your entire life, to do this.* You now have a completely clean slate on which to create your basic lifestyle. Once you commit yourself to a luxury, or more likely several luxuries, it is almost impossible to go back again to the basics and rethink. We're all human, and we rapidly adopt a standard for our lifestyles that is extremely difficult to lower unless we are forced to do so by some traumatic reversal of fortune. This is the only time in your life when you can establish this benchmark free of previously established, and increasing, expectations. So take this exercise seriously and, trust me, you'll be very glad you did.

Saving and Investing

Before making your luxury decisions, though, another task needs attention. You need to save. Notice, I didn't say it was a good idea to save, or that you should save. I said you need to save. This is the part of financial management that equates to the time you spend building more depth and breadth into your professional knowledge base. Let's look at why.

Basically, the two reasons are that someday you will want to be rich and that in between, stuff happens. It's always possible that you will win the lottery, or that you will someday be a key part of the management team of a start-up that will make you rich. But, the vast, overwhelming majority of us do not experience either of these windfalls. So the odds are stacked heavily against you. No, if you want to be rich, you're going to have to start now and do it the hard way. The fact is that the vast majority of us who have created the wealth to retire comfortably and enjoy the mental calm that comes from knowing we're financially secure have done so by saving, and not by striking it rich or by investing. The first is not going to happen, and investing only gives us the opportunity to make more out of what we set aside, but that doesn't help us if nothing's been set aside. The fact is that it is far harder to save than it is to grow our savings through our investments.

Remember the times earlier in the book that we talked about building good habits early? Well, the habit of saving may be the most important of all. At this stage in your career, it almost doesn't make any difference how much you save. The really important thing is just that you do save and that you do so regularly. After you have established the habit of regular, uninterrupted, undisturbed saving, the amounts will take care of themselves. You will see that you are building up an investment base, you will watch it grow, and you will get great satisfaction from knowing that you're being good to yourself.

This investment base will take a long time to amount to what you might consider real money. It's like an airplane taking off. It stays on the ground for a long time, building speed very gradually. Then, the nose wheel slowly lifts off the ground to a modest angle. Finally, the main landing gear is clear and the angle of attack increases more. At this point, it's not very impressive given the goals of 30,000 feet and 500 miles per hour. But then speed and altitude begin to increase geometrically, breathtakingly. So it goes with your savings program. Like the airplane achieving the stratosphere, one day you'll be amazed at what you've created.

One more thought. See if your employer has a payroll deduction savings plan that will take the amount of your choice directly from your salary and deposit it for you. You'll appreciate the fact that you won't have to see this money every month and rely on your own self-discipline to get it to the bank yourself. Don't give yourself the opportunity to be tempted or forgetful.

In the Navy, all of us were urged to establish a monthly allotment for U. S. Savings Bonds. Without really thinking about it, I signed up for some nominal amount, probably $25 or so to begin with. Then I forgot it, literally. When I was released four years later, I was stunned to realize I had several thousand dollars set aside; quite a large sum of money at that particular time in my life.

If your employer has a 401(k) plan or similar retirement savings vehicle that provides for voluntary employee contributions, use it. Its annual growth will not be reduced by taxes, and the restrictions on withdrawal that accompany these plans add another layer of protection against occasional lapses in self-discipline.

If you need an additional incentive to save, think of the down payment that you'll need one day for your first house. Historically, owning a single-family home has been one of the most consistently productive means for most of us to build wealth. Investing your hard-won savings in residential real estate is usually a great decision. And having an adequate down payment is often a huge challenge for first-time home buyers.

Saving for Unknowns

Recognize at this point that you have two important savings tasks. Saving for wealth building was discussed above.

The second is saving for the bumps in the road that all of us experience from time to time. The death of a car will take big bucks. A family illness may result in medical bills not covered by insurance, or require an unusual amount of travel. Any number of things can unexpectedly drain your cash reserves.

There are two ways to be prepared for this. In creating your own financial management plan, you can simply provide a certain amount each month for contingencies. In your mind, you've already spent this money so you don't miss it. Then, at the end of the year, if emergencies didn't eat it up, you have a nice surprise and a bigger holiday trip.

Some people, though, actually place their contingency funds in separate bank accounts in order to have them physically set aside. This is a particularly good idea if you feel you may need help in the self-discipline department. One advantage is that when the account reaches the level that you feel is adequate to cover any feasible contingency, you can simply stop adding to it until it needs replenishment. A cautionary note, however. If you do this, don't put your contingency savings in the same account as your investment savings. That account needs to stay completely undisturbed.

How much will you need to cover contingencies? That varies for reasons of family, geography, environment, etc. Experience will tell you, but until it does, try 10% of all other non-discretionary spending. Also, consider the age of your car. Automobiles are often the source of unexpected costs. If yours is older, set aside more for contingencies. If it is new, you won't need as much, particularly if it is still under warranty.

Luxury Spending

Finally we get to the part where you get to live the good life. So just how good will it be? Start with your expected income, subtract your mandatory spending, your contingency and investment savings, and what you have left is the answer. Now, look at that want list for luxuries and find good estimates of the associated costs. If you have rank ordered the list and you're confident in those decisions, then it's just a matter of working down the list until you've spent all your available discretionary income.

Few of us are so lucky, however. Most of us have to juggle and jiggle, retool estimates to apply more modest expectations, and consider really difficult trade-offs. It's not easy. Most of us have wants that are beyond our means, but most of us usually do a pretty good job of sorting that out into responsible but still satisfying spending plans. And consider how you'll be saving the ones you can't afford now for later, which gives you something to look forward to. My grandfather (who was my first mentor) often counseled me to "save the best for last." I've found a lot of satisfaction and pleasure in following his advice.

The Real Cost of Debt

The opportunity to borrow money is a critical ingredient in our American way of life. A great deal of our economy and standard of living directly dependents upon it. But excessive debt is a truly destructive force that can ruin our ability to enjoy our lifestyles. Responsibly used, borrowing can permit purchases that we couldn't otherwise make. We pay for these products while we use them rather than having to wait until we have the purchase price in hand.

Sounds very reasonable. Carried beyond our ability to comfortably pay them back, however, these same debts can grind us down and ruin our ability to function effectively from day to day.

My father graduated from college in the middle of America's Great Depression. His father had lost everything because his business was unable to repay its relatively modest debts when its revenues were decimated by the economy of that era. My dad never forgot the devastating effect of his father's and others' unpayable debt. As a result, he never again borrowed money, except for a small mortgage that facilitated the purchase of our family's home. And even then, it seemed like he couldn't work hard enough to repay it. He simply slept better knowing that he owed "nothing to nobody."

Dad's story represents an extreme, and I'm not suggesting otherwise. But it illustrates just how much pain he witnessed when his father's income suddenly became insufficient to repay debts that seemed even conservative only a short while before. He was not alone. Throughout my business career, I've had a number of clients with similar stories, and a similar fear of virtually any debt at all.

Today, a surprising portion of our population owes more on credit card debt than can be repaid out of near-term earnings. This happens for the simple reason that our current business practices make it easy to buy an amazing array of goods and services on credit. Many people have spent considerable sums on purchases that they simply would not have made if they had had to go the bank and arrange a loan first. The unfortunate consequence of this is that they pay rates of interest and related charges far in excess of what would result from a bank loan. So they borrow, in many cases, unneeded funds and then pay extremely high costs to carry the loan. This may be beneficial to the economy, but can be devastating to the individuals involved.

Personal bankruptcies have been on the rise for much of my adult life, largely as a result of credit card borrowing to fund marginally needed purchases. It's not unusual, we are told, for required payments on these balances to consume the majority of an individual's paycheck for years. Imagine the empty feeling that would surely result from making payments for years on items that have long since lost their utility to the purchaser. Imagine also the disposable income consumed by service charges and high rates of interest that mean only a fraction of any payment actually reduces the amount owed. Then imagine living this way for years, compromising your ability to purchase really-needed products and services. People who find themselves in this situation frequently report the inability to pay for medical services for their families.

As bad as this sounds, the real cost of high levels of debt is often emotional. Living one step ahead of the bill collector consumes a great deal of energy and time, arguably our only real assets. People in this situation report spending startling portions of their workdays dealing with the negative effects—and when not dealing with them, worrying about them. They are often significantly less productive than their co-workers, making them more vulnerable to missed promotions and layoffs. In a seminar recently, one woman who had suffered under this burden and finally managed to work her way out from under it openly wept as she related the feeling of freedom she now enjoys compared to the prison she found herself in for years.

Is debt bad? It's like many other things–that depends on how we use it. The point is to move carefully and consider the level at which you will commit future income for present-day satisfactions. Impulsive debt-financed purchases are almost always avoided at all costs by people who enjoy the freedom of financial independence.

Personal Money Management

"Budget" is an interesting word. It carries a lot of baggage that causes most of us to place it alongside taxes in our picture of our financial independence. "Financial plan," however, is a very current and almost sophisticated concept that projects a certain responsible panache. Use whichever you like; they're the same thing. Either way, you need one. Follow the kind of financial plan detailed earlier and you will be happy you did, because it will lead you to financial independence, which is one great feeling.

Budgeting is a discipline. It's not unlike training for an athletic event. It involves doing mundane, routine things every day to promote your ability to compete effectively and win the game. In your physical training routine, you probably play little mind games with yourself to overcome the boredom and get a few more reps out of strained, tired muscles. Do the same with your financial plan. Find ways to trick yourself into doing what you know you need to do. It's not unlike a person who's perpetually late setting her clock ahead by ten minutes. Looking at that clock, her mind tells her that it's ten minutes fast, and yet that emotional impact of seeing herself about to be late helps her stay on schedule.

The corresponding budget trick might be to periodically subtract a targeted savings amount from your checkbook even though you haven't actually removed the money. Logically, you know it's still in there, but emotionally you are moved to respect the balance that shows up in your check register. The ultimate financial mind game, of course, is the system of maintaining envelopes for all mandatory monthly expenditures. On payday, the envelopes are filled with the required amounts, and are then emptied during the month to pay the bills as they come due. Whatever is left over after the envelopes are filled represents disposable income for that period. Few of us have to resort to this extreme, but if this works for you, use it. After all, it's likely that no one but you will ever know.

The Feeling of Financial Discipline

If you buy the advice offered in previous chapters, you have a career plan that will move you toward your goals. You'll revisit it periodically, adjust some of the components to account for the progress you've made and the things you've learned. You may even throw it out and start over at some point. If you also happen to be a serious athlete, you will have a training plan that you use in much the same way. For all the same reasons, you need to have a financial plan that addresses your own personal needs.

Your career plan permits you to know where you are in your professional growth, to see what's ahead, and to adjust as necessary. More than that, it allows you to take pride in the effort you put into your career and the progress that effort yields. It allows you to celebrate, to know that you are accomplishing something very important for yourself. Use your financial plan in this way.

Most people don't do this. Most of us in the United States were raised in an environment of relative plenty. Money was a facilitating mechanism that, while perhaps not always abundant, was at least never in truly short supply. We took it for granted. Can we expect this environment of plenty to continue into the future? Who knows. The likelihood, however, is that it will not continue to grow at the rates seen in the past generation or so, and may even suffer significant reversals from time to time. Those with their eye on future financial objectives and who employ a disciplined approach to regularly moving the ball toward those objectives will see a much more secure future and be much better able to weather any storms along the way.

A well-conceived and well-executed financial plan will provide great personal satisfaction as you meet your financial goals. Celebrate progress and evaluate setbacks just as you do with your career plan. And remember, *you will likely never have a better time in your entire life to set this course with fewer conflicts than you do right now.*

13

Professional and Business Ethics

Ethics are secular rules of conduct. Unlike morals, which have their foundation in religious belief, ethics usually have to do with the smooth functioning of a segment of society. Recent corporate disasters illustrate the fact that failures of business and professional ethics regularly ruin careers and hurt innocent bystanders. This chapter highlights the importance of ethics in a professional career along with the mind-set needed to build on this foundation.

Professional Ethics

Virtually every recognized profession has a body of ethics that governs its conduct on a day to day basis. In addition, these same professions are usually regulated by individual states, which also have bodies of rules. These two rule books often overlap within a particular jurisdiction, but seldom conflict. Since the states grant professional licenses to practice (and can revoke them), licensing authorities put real teeth into each state's rules of professional conduct. The rules of professional societies are often even more stringent than the states' rules.

Each month, most state regulatory bodies report numerous suspensions or restrictions of the right to practice of practitioners found to have violated their rules. That can be a career ender–but even if not, it can cut a professional's earning power for an extended period. Non-governmental professional societies exercise similar rights, but their actions are usually limited to expulsion from the society itself, a blow to the professional's credibility but not necessarily his career.

These rules of professional conduct, or ethics, have grown out of two needs. The buyers of professional services need protection from professional misconduct; the professionals need the public to trust that they are competent. It is usually very difficult for a buyer of professional services to know whether he is getting a quality product. The professions involve large bodies of esoteric knowledge that are not ordinarily available to, or even understandable by the general public. How do you know if your attorney is delivering quality legal advice? You may like him a lot; you may inherently trust him; you may see him as a pillar of your community. But how do you evaluate the quality of his professional services? Most people have no means to do this, short of hiring another attorney to do quality control. This is where the states come in. They provide legislative and regulatory standards by which the professions are evaluated, often by boards consisting, at least in part, of other members of the same profession.

Maintaining a high level of public trust is as important to the professions as it is to the buying public. Professional services often, perhaps ordinarily, involve client matters of extreme sensitivity. An architect's faulty design risks the lives of hundreds of owners and users, and hurts the contiguous properties. Bad legal advice on how to structure the estate of a client can result in higher taxes and unintended asset distributions. A consultant advising on the restructuring of a large corporation may be compromising the livelihoods of hundreds of its employees.

All of these services require unusually high levels of confidence between the client and the professional delivering them. By establishing and maintaining standards of conduct that surpass those required of others in the community, professions support the public confidence necessary to facilitate continuing demand for their services.

The content of bodies of ethical standards is similar from one profession to another. Most involve variations on the following themes:

- **SERVICE STANDARDS.** Definitions of minimum acceptable levels of quality for the services delivered by the profession usually begin by stressing the need to place the client's interests first. Other elements might relate to the competence of the practitioner and the appropriateness of the services offered to the client's needs.

- **PUBLIC INTEREST.** Whether directly stated or not, most establish the public good as an essential element of the profession's reason for being. This, then, is the basis upon which the state will grant a practice license to an individual. Compromise of the public interest is often the basis upon which a license is revoked for malpractice. This is the foundation for such things as the independence of Certified Public Accountants and the concept of attorneys being agents of the court.

- **RULES OF COMPETITION.** These standards usually have to do with such things as misrepresentations in dealings with clients, charging reasonable fees, and the like. Until the 1970s, prohibitions against such things as advertising by professionals such as CPAs and attorneys, and the recruiting of fellow professionals' employees were also common. Most of these rules have now been deemed to restrain trade and have been repealed.

- **RELATIONS WITH CLIENTS.** Most provide quite detailed rules governing the relationships between professionals and their clients. This often has to do with such things as the ownership of work product, the confidentiality of client information, and the reasonableness of fees.

The bottom line, whatever your profession, is that you will be expected to know and observe the ethical standards promulgated by your professional society and by the state in which you practice.

Ethics in Business

The ethics of professional practice tend to be very clearly stated and universally understood. In the realm of general business practice, however, the concept of ethics becomes much fuzzier and many of the enforcement mechanisms of states and professional societies is lacking. Nevertheless, the concept has great relevance and is often very important to the public perception of many businesses. As the professions are also businesses, these rules must be respected as well.

The ethical conduct of business is often hard to define, but is inextricably linked to the American concepts of fair play and level playing field. While hard and fast rules are difficult to come by here, your strongest tools are a sound system of values and good judgment. A win-win orientation is helpful, and the Golden Rule is not a bad guide in the absence of more precise guidelines. Greed, ego, and one-sided self-interest are your enemies.

In a general sense, professional rules of conduct are easier to follow than ethical guidelines because of their specificity and the clear consequences of breaking them.

One of the most poignant pieces of advice I ever received was meant to relate to professional conduct, but has also provided a wonderful guide to ethical matters in general. I once had a partner who was more a grandfather figure to me than a mentor. He was already a partner somewhere when I was born. One day we discussed a particularly difficult situation in which my client want-

ed to take a too-aggressive position on a tax matter. I was very uncomfortable with the situation. The client was clearly pushing the limit and was very determined. I was unsure about how to proceed without risking my relationship with a very good client. My experience-wise partner said, "John, it's OK to drive in the street. Occasionally, it's even OK to drive on the shoulder, but it's never OK to drive on the sidewalk. You get paid to tell your client where he's driving, and if you don't do it, then you're not earning the fees he's paying you." He was right! I went and had that conversation, despite the well-recognized tendency of many tax consulting clients to shoot the messenger. It was a tough conversation; my client was not happy. Our relationship continued for many years, however, and I believe it became stronger for the stand I took.

Like the application of the tax law, the practice of business ethics is often a matter of judgment. You might think that this makes the system more malleable, more flexible. In one sense you'd be right. It's usually easier to stretch the limits and boundaries of business ethics. Thus, we give our business colleagues more latitude here, and this undoubtedly produces more marginal behavior, more "driving on the shoulder." It's not at all hard to look around and observe business practices, sometimes even within our own firms, that we would personally choose to avoid.

In a larger sense, however, those who push the boundaries of business ethics too often or too far can pay an even harsher price than the occasionally errant professional. Business is a matter of trust. Documenting contractual obligations can mitigate some of the trust risk in a relationship, but the fundamental element in most business transactions, documentation notwithstanding, is the trust shared by two or more human beings who each pledge to do something that will contribute to an outcome that will be mutually beneficial. These people are looking for others with a history of doing what they've committed to do, and treating fairly those with whom they deal. Thus, one's ethical practices are continually being observed and noted, even if not consciously. And they are remembered.

The consequences of failures of business ethics can be subtle and far reaching. A bad reputation can damage an individual's ability to function in the business community for years, sometimes without the individual recognizing its influence.

And individuals with reputations for unethical behavior often wake up to find that they're surrounded by others like themselves—clients and co-workers whose ethical behavior is also questionable. I've often wondered if this is simply a matter of like kinds attracting one another or perhaps results from their having closed off better relationships because of their own behavior. I'm not certain just why this happens, but I know that it does. I think others usually see this same phenomenon, which helps explain why we are often known by the company we keep—whether we like it or not.

It seems to me that the true essence of ethical behavior is simply a matter of respect. The more fully we respect those with whom we come in contact, the greater our motivation to fulfill our commitments to them and to treat them fairly. A natural extension of this is to respect ourselves. The more we do, the less we tolerate unethical behavior in ourselves.

Ethics and You

Discussions of ethical behavior can be pretty intangible. If you're like most, you are starting your career fully expecting to play by the rules and assuming that those rules will be fair and reasonably clear. In practice, however, the choices are usually not between black and white, and the implications of your choices can be fuzzy and not obvious until after the fact.

The best advice I can give is to be diligent but reasonable. The diligent part comes from giving regular attention to the ethics of your own profession. You will probably have a good start here if you are in a regulated profession, as ethics are a common subject in licensing examinations. After that, you will almost certainly see changes to these rules reported in professional publications. The time required for you to read about these changes will probably be minimal, but should provide you with a periodic reminder of where things stand. Reading about disciplinary actions against errant fellow practitioners will also provide good input. Minimal time is required here.

Following the general business press (if the past couple of years are any guide) should likewise provide you with plenty to think about on the subject of general business ethics. The point here is to find your own way to keep your ethical perspective current in terms of the state of the rules and the situations that others are encountering.

The part about being reasonable relates to your application of what you know. I can assure you that you will regularly encounter situations that will present ethical issues. You might observe a client's employee misappropriating office supplies. Or a supervisor might ask you to charge more time to a project than you actually worked. In contrast, the request might be for less time in order to stay within a budget. Perhaps a colleague reports a travel expense that wasn't actually incurred. And occasionally, you may encounter a matter with far larger consequences. As an auditor, I once discovered a forged document that involved many thousands of dollars.

Your choice involves how to respond when you see things that you believe violate basic rules of ethical behavior. While I don't mean to suggest that the business world is full of ethically challenged people (in fact, my experience is quite the opposite), the fact is that ethical violations are fairly common. Most, however, are of very little real consequence in the overall scheme of things. So you must decide where your own personal tolerance level lies.

You might decide, for example, that you will go along with your supervisor when he first asks you to add a small amount to the time you report. At some point, however, because it happens too many times or involves more than just a minimal number of hours, you may decide that you can no longer comply. Then it becomes a matter of what you do about the situation.

One good approach is to ask, in a non-judgmental way, why this is happening. You might find that there really is an explanation that doesn't involve an ethical issue. Or you might find that in just asking the question you put a spotlight on the practice and thereby cause it to go away. If neither of these results, then you must find your own way to communicate that you can no longer go along. Your best approach is always to avoid personalizing the matter.

It's not about the individual, it's about the act. This is also good practice for learning to say the word no, something too few people are comfortable doing.

Think this can be a tough conversation? You're right, it can. Which just points out the fact that you need to be quite certain that you want to take on the issue before you get into it. My advice is to pick your battles—you can't fight them all.

Firm Interests vs. Client Interests

As the professions have become less regulated over the past decade or two, most have diversified their service offerings. In the public accounting world where I spent a good deal of my career, the evolution of management consulting typifies this trend. Early in my career, our consulting division adopted the slogan, "Strive for Five," meaning five percent of our firm's total revenues. When I left the firm more than twenty-five years later, consulting's portion of total revenue was approaching fifty percent, and its portfolio of services included many that had not even existed at the beginning. Along with this trend came an enormous effort to cross-sell those services to existing clients.

Cross-selling capitalizes on the knowledge that partners and staff gain about their clients' business operations (or personal situations in the cases of individual clients) and leverages that knowledge to identify client needs for additional services. When a firm identifies a client's additional needs, and introduces a new specialist who has a good understanding of the client's business, the firm can often sell additional services without the client even considering another provider. This helps to build bench strength in service capability without the relatively high marketing costs that might otherwise be required.

If you are asked to look for cross-selling opportunities within your group of clients, you may feel that you are being placed squarely in the middle of a dilemma. You are being asked to use knowledge that your client may consider confidential to identify opportunities for your firm to sell additional services. But is this a problem?

First, consider who owns the client relationship. In every large firm that I know of, the client belongs to the firm, and not to the individual professional who provides its services at any particular point in time. Thus, it ordinarily follows ("ordinarily" because many of these rules vary from state to state) that the confidentiality rules do not apply to the flow of information within the firm itself.

Second, consider whether the client will be better off if it receives these new services. This relates to the extent of client need, the competence of the specialists who will provide the service, and the value proposition involved.

Frankly, this issue gave me pause on occasion. As a partner, often the principal partner assigned to the client, I had to assess the probability that the new services would provide a level of value that would enhance my relationship with the client, and thereby strengthen the client's loyalty to my firm.

On occasion, I was not happy with the odds, feeling that because of the newness of the service capability or my reservations about the competence level

*of those who would provide the service, there was
a significant possibility that the overall result would
not be positive. In the few situations where this
happened, I passed. I didn't raise the possibility
with either my client or my firm even though it
would have been in my immediate interest to sell
the new service.*

*I believe that in the few instances where this hap-
pened, I made the right decision for my firm, feeling
that the client relationship was a more valuable
asset than the potential revenue from selling the
service. As the relationship manager, I felt it was my
responsibility to maintain a happy, loyal client. But it
was never an easy call, and I might have been quite
legitimately criticized for those decisions.*

The Hazards of Litigation

The "hazards of litigation" is a phrase you will hear frequently in many professions these days. It is very descrip-
tive—litigation is hazardous. The rule of law prevails in
the United States as in almost no other country in the
world. It probably works, in part, because it is so often
practiced. Plaintiffs' attorneys commonly take on the
mightiest of our institutions, starting with our Federal
government itself. And they are frequently very successful and therefore highly compensated. But the attorneys
who defend these institutions are good too, with the
result that business-related litigation can be a lengthy
and bitter process.

In the broad picture, the opportunities that our courts afford to redress grievances serve us very well. The system prevents many of the unfair and unproductive business practices that constrain many other economies of the world. But in a smaller view, litigation can be terribly unproductive for the companies involved. It can sap the energy of those who are directly involved by diverting their attention away from the things that make them and their companies successful. Nowhere is this truer than in a professional services firm where time is, quite literally, money.

Typically, when a firm is sued over some aspect of its service to a client, the partners (and often others as well) are forced to spend a great deal of time dealing with it. This usually involves recovering and reviewing pertinent records, conferences with the firm's attorneys, depositions by other parties, monitoring the testimony of others, and court appearances. In addition to losing time, the firm can lose focus during this period.

Professionals usually take great pride in their work. When the quality or value of that work is questioned, it can drain energy and divert attention like few other of life's most severe crises. You have been wounded. Productivity suffers. Your head is somewhere else, even when your body is present.

For this reason, most professional firms have come to realize that settling litigation as soon as possible is often the best response. Those involved are able to get back to work and regain lost productivity. This route is usually taken in all but the cases that seriously threaten the firm's professional reputation, involve a great deal of money, or can be efficiently and effectively defended.

Professional firms increasingly seek to avoid the hazards of litigation through the use of binding arbitration. In this non-judicial process, a knowledgeable arbitrator is agreed upon, hears the facts presented by the parties, and renders a resolution that each side has agreed in advance will conclude the matter. Rules of evidence and testimony are much more relaxed than in the courts. Ordinarily, judicial appeal is not available. This is a tricky process with its own set of hazards, but compared with the time and energy required to litigate, and considering the risks of entrusting complex business litigation to relatively unsophisticated juries, arbitration offers some compelling value and will likely continue to do so.

14

Client Confidentiality

In some professions, the confidentiality of client information is prescribed by professional standards of conduct. It's the law. But in all professions, it is a good idea. Here's why.

Matters Requiring Confidentiality

I have a friend who thinks nothing of discussing his compensation and other financial information with just about anyone who'll listen. I, on the other hand, summarily dis-

156   Professional Success—Chapter 14

card any marketing inquiry that asks for even general information about my income. That's my business, not theirs.
The point is that everyone has his or her own sensitivities
to things they consider confidential, and what's unimportant to one person may be highly important to another.

When it comes to clients, these sensitivities often involve
things of great magnitude, and therefore even greater sensitivities. The estate plan being crafted by an attorney necessarily involves a comprehensive picture of her client's
wealth. The investment decisions being made by that same
client's money manager may involve all of his liquid assets.
And an architect must be in on some of the most intimate
strategic plans of her corporate client as she considers the
use of the space she has been retained to design.

Each of these professional practitioners is in a position of
great trust—and can do great damage if she treats information about her client casually and either knowingly or
unknowingly shares it with others. The damage may be real
or only imagined, but that's totally up to the client to determine. And even though you may think you know, you can
never really be sure where your client's sensitivity level lies.

Some professions are more attuned to client confidentiality than others. Financial matters have historically
scored very high on the sensitivity scale. As a result, my
professional career as an accountant has prepared me well
for this subject.

---

*Early in my career, I was assigned to several proj-
ects for one of the most prominent and wealthy
families in the community. I was often privy to
transactions, either under consideration or under*

way, that could have had a significant impact on
the community. As a result of several experiences
when I was forced to choose between alienating a
curious friend who knew of my involvement with
this particular family and compromising client con-
fidentiality, I adopted a rule that has served me
well over the years. I simply do not disclose who
my clients are to others, usually not even my wife.

This is not always easy or convenient. One place where revealing client relationships can be particularly helpful is in written proposals for new clients and projects. Having clients with important names in the community, and revealing those names when attempting to win new clients, can be a real credibility builder. Before naming clients in a proposal or conversation with a prospect, I first check with my client. Most are glad to help out and only too happy to have their name connected with mine. Occasionally, however, a client will request that I not do so. On the rare occasions where this happens, I have to respect his priorities. After all, my first priority is to my existing client who has already demonstrated his confidence in my abilities and paid me real money.

On one such occasion, this request produced a
startling result. I phoned the CEO of an important
client of my firm to ask if I could refer to our very
good relationship in a proposal for a potential new
client. After asking the name of my prospect, the

man agreed but then went on to advise me quite casually that he was happy for my firm to work for him or my prospect, whichever I chose. First, I was simply speechless, then very disappointed. Finally, I was angry. But as I came to realize, better to discover the issue at that point than after winning my new client—only to lose my highly valued existing one.

If you are entering the practice of law or medicine, you will find even higher sensitivity levels regarding the confidentiality of client information. Each has its own unique application of the general rule, but the consequences of disclosure can be every bit as severe as in the accounting profession. Financial planning and money management are also areas where confidentiality is considered to be a hallmark of professionalism, although the related rules are not quite so well-developed.

The best possible advice on this subject is to learn the rules of your profession and then go out of your way to exceed their requirements. Your clients will respect you for it, and the benefits of keeping your mouth shut will far exceed any transitory popularity you may enjoy because of the inside knowledge that you possess.

So What Can I Say About My Clients?

I believe the best policy is to say nothing that can be identified with a particular company or individual directly. After I made the decision to simply tell no one who my clients were, my life and my cocktail conversations became a lot easier. Of course, if you are serving a publicly owned corporation, your firm's client relationship may be a matter of public record. Then your choice becomes whether to let it be known that you are personally involved and how.

This is not to say, however, that you shouldn't talk about your clients. Just make sure that what you say is generic enough to not be related back to the particular client or project. The opportunity, and in fact the need, to talk about your practice and the work you do is very important in developing new clients for your firm and broadening your relationships with existing clients. Your ability to relate the things you've done to help others will help you expand your practice and grow your firm. You need to do this well. Find ways to tell interesting stories taken from your professional work and you will find the most effective means to help others understand what you do, and to appreciate you for the professional that you are. Just do it in ways that don't reveal, even indirectly, information that a sensitive client might feel it was your responsibility to protect.

15

Communication
That Works

Without a doubt, the most common complaint that I've
heard from partners about their staffs is that they write
badly. I have a lot of questions about this statement. I won-
der, for example, whether this reflects a basic problem in
our educational process, or whether the problem is just so
in-your-face when it exists. I suspect the latter. And this is
why it's a problem you don't want to have.

Professional Writing is Professional

The world of professional services is populated by many of the best-educated and brightest people in the world. Many other cultures attract an even higher percentage of their elite to the professions than does the United States. In this environment, where intelligence and education are so highly prized, a professional's ability to communicate with his peers, and with the public in general, is a hallmark of professionalism. Being published is an important part of demonstrating an individual's value in the professional community. Written communications are often directly integral to success, as with the court filings of the attorney or the financial statement footnotes of the professional accountant.

In our professional world, where such value is placed on written communications, nothing—and I mean nothing—stands out quite so immediately and dramatically as bad writing. And in standing out so immediately, almost nothing (that I can think of at least) speaks so negatively about the individual behind it.

Gordon Houseman, for example, had it all. I could see that within days after I hired him as an experienced tax consultant. As I watched him meet and work with clients, I saw an individual with a real gift for many of the key success factors in our business. He was personable and approachable. He knew his area of the tax law very thoroughly. And he had that unique ability that is so often missing—he could connect the dots, by relating needs to solutions for clients. I was truly impressed—that is, until I read something he'd written.

Gordon clearly did not have a command of the written word. Some of his sentences lacked key structural elements. Some failed to complete a thought. In some, it looked as though he had scattered a handful of commas like birdseed, completely without intent. Others had virtually no punctuation at all, and simply rambled on for line after line as if desperately looking for a way to commit suicide and end it all.

Gordon's writing presented two real puzzlers for me. First of all, Gordon was an adjunct professor at a local university, and had been for a number of years. How, I wondered, could he have landed this position in an arena that, perhaps above all others, should place great value on effective writing? And once hired, how could he effectively evaluate the performance of his students, which was so often demonstrated through the written word, when he so lacked the necessary ability himself? This line of questioning brought me eventually to lose respect for the institution for which he taught.

And therein lies the problem for you if you also lack the necessary skill to communicate effectively in writing. It will reflect badly not only on you, but also on your firm. For your firm's clients will read what you write. And those clients, just like me, will begin to question the professionalism of you and your firm. Needless to say, your employer will not look kindly on this result. In fact, it will go to great lengths to assure that it doesn't happen, which brings us back to where we started, with partner comments about staff who can't write. It's a real problem.

The other puzzler presented by Gordon's bad writing was that he didn't speak that way. Orally, he was very well put together and professional. Why is this contrast puzzling? Because in my experience, those who write badly are often simply parroting their way of speaking. This is probably another reason why bad writing evokes such negative reactions. If you are first introduced to someone through his written communications, as frequently happens, and if that writing happens to be bad, you form a negative impression about him. However erroneous that impression might be, it is very difficult to overcome. You assume that a person's writing is a reflection of his way of speaking.

This relationship between the written and spoken word suggests that the solution to bad writing may lie to some extent in correcting people's grammar when they speak. It also suggests the value of reading what you've written—aloud. I sometimes use a hand-held tape recorder for this purpose, but usually I just listen as I read.

You try it. Pause for commas and periods, raise your inflection for question marks, and be emphatic for exclamation marks. How do you like the sound of what you've written? Is it intelligent? Well put together? Representative of the professional you seek to be? If not, correct the writing and speak it again. This makes so much sense to me that I'm often surprised that others don't do it as a matter of course. This was part of the solution for Gordon when he was eventually persuaded to address the problem.

Effective business communication is often stifled by the overly formal and structured use of business-speak. To me this term captures all of those words and phrases that business people use in an attempt to demonstrate control over others or show their importance through the use of power language. Sometimes, though, it indicates nothing beyond a particularly dull and uncreative personality.

If you want to see what I mean, find a business journal that regularly profiles business leaders' views and observations about themselves and their businesses. You often see questions like, "What is your most important business principal?" or "How do you keep a competitive edge?" Read about a half dozen of these and you'll notice how all of the answers sound the same. They really communicate very little beyond the catch phrases of the day. They serve, I suppose, to confirm the executive's connection with the latest thinking on business leadership.

Look long enough, however, and you'll find a very few of these that communicate an openness and sense of reality that immediately gets your attention. Occasionally, you come away feeling as if you really have learned something about the individual—that you know her. The freshness of these (and their scarcity, perhaps) invariably causes me to feel a connection with this person and a certain respect for her honesty and openness. I'd work for her, and I'd probably never have any doubt about where I stood or about what was important to her.

Speaking Well

Speaking well is as necessary for a professional as is effective writing. The need comes with the job. Your credibility as a professional will depend on it. Speaking represents your opportunity to raise your profile with your peers and the community in general. When you speak to a group of people who came to hear you, you establish yourself as a leader and as an authority on your subject. Both of these credentials are critical elements in your ability to succeed as a professional.

Everyone can learn to speak well. Like any art, it will come naturally to some, while others will struggle to gain the necessary ground through hard work and practice. I am not a natural speaker. I'm not particularly attractive or funny. I don't have a voice with oratorical resonance. But I've become a reasonably decent speaker because I had to.

Everyone has stories to tell about learning to speak as a professional, and these stories often contain valuable lessons. So I'll relate some of the things that have contributed to my development at the podium:

- RELAX. Sounds easy for me to say, right? The thought of speaking to a group is the very definition of anxiety for many, and it certainly was for me at one time. In fact, I attribute virtually all of my failures as a speaker to being wooden and frozen in place. I had that deer in the headlights look, and I'm sure my audiences felt sorry for me. They wanted it to be over as much as I did. When I finally learned to relax, my performances got better in a hurry.

  Accomplishing this was easy—once I learned the secret. I learned to smile. Not the phony, painted-on sort of smile that is only one step away from screaming, "I want out of here." No, I mean smiling from within, really open-your-soul smiling that's obviously genuine. An authentic smile from within draws people to me as I know it does for others as well. And drawing the audience to me with the reciprocated warmth of a genuine smile allows me to relax and really communicate.

So how do I muster up one of these genuine smiles when I'm petrified? Sometimes I remember a favorite touching scene from a movie. Sometimes I think of a really tender family moment. Sometimes I recall a really funny thing that happened with a friend. And sometimes I am able to just reach down inside and be warmed by the realization that I am unique in the whole world and am here before this group for a purpose.

■ **TALK TO SOMEONE IN PARTICULAR.** It always helps when you can tell that you're communicating with a person—really making points that are meaningful, really educating if that's the purpose (as it often is when professionals make presentations). I often realize after a few minutes, in fact, that several people in the audience are really into what I'm saying, and that I'm unconsciously talking to them individually. As this realization dawns, I focus on bringing others into the fold. Often this works and others connect up with me. Sometimes it doesn't, and I move on. But speaking to an individual rather than a faceless group helps me to be more real, more communicative.

Another technique that I try to work into all of my presentations is to meet several people in the audience before the presentation. This puts an essentially institutional function, my presentation, on a personal level before it begins. It gives me some faces to talk to when I begin, and they seem to connect with what I'm saying more quickly than might otherwise be the case.

- **KNOW YOUR SUBJECT.** Nothing brings me back to a state of anxiety faster than the thought that I don't know my subject. What if someone in the audience sees through me, sees that I really don't know what I'm talking about? What if someone asks a question that I can't answer, particularly if I should know it? Some experienced speakers are very casual about being in this predicament. They parry the thrust of the question with deft skill, sometimes even seeming to leave the audience with the impression that the question was not even worth asking. I have seldom been this effective in this situation. Someone once told me to simply remember that I know more about my subject than anyone else in the audience. This has never made total sense to me, but it has helped me on occasion to trick myself into a state of semi-calm. But for me, the secret here has been content preparation along with anticipation of my audience. If I prepare thoroughly, I do fine.

- **ORGANIZE YOUR PRESENTATION.** Tell them what you're going to say, then say it, and then tell them what you said. This piece of advice seems to show up wherever you see suggestions for public speakers. It sounds boring and uncreative, but it works. Framing the content of a presentation beforehand seems to help people get into it and find their place earlier on. Sometimes it's not appropriate, but often it is. And recapping always helps, particularly after a long involved subject.

- **BEWARE OF VISUAL AIDS.** Don't put all of your presentation on the screen and then read it to the audience. Absolutely nothing good can come of this. When visuals are clearly required, I like to list major points only and then review and discuss them, all with a great deal of ad-libbing. If I'm presenting something that people will want to take home with them, then I always try to give them copies of my visual aids, leaving plenty of room for them to make notes if they choose. The tendency to load up your screens has still another downside. They are often unreadable, particularly by those in the back of the room. The result is that you find your audience struggling to read all the words on your screens and ignoring the words you're speaking. Not exactly consistent with your reason for being there in the first place.

- **DON'T TRY TO TELL A JOKE UNLESS YOU'RE FUNNY.** An attempt at humor that falls flat is an absolutely terrible way to start a speech. I know. I've certainly done it enough. I have found, though, that if I'm truly relaxed and if the joke is one that I truly find funny, it always relaxes everyone (me included) if I tell it. It then becomes truly a matter of my sharing something that is meaningful to me, and the audience can easily relate to that and appreciate it even if people don't find the joke humorous.

   I've also found that funny stories, particularly stories about myself, work better for me than jokes, which usually have an inauthentic quality when I try to tell them. Self-effacing stories about myself also serve another purpose. They help the audience believe that I don't take myself too seriously. Then we can all relax.

One final point about jokes–don't tell off-color stories. They're a loaded gun. Some people can consistently pull this off, but I can't and the chances are that if you're wondering if you can or not, you can't either. Further, the vast majority are unprofessional and will detract from rather than enhance your image, even when they are funny.

Practice, practice, practice

Flat-water racing shells are very delicate vessels, and rowing them well requires the mastery and coordinated use of a number of different elements. The rowing stroke is every bit as complex as a golf swing or a basketball lay-up in traffic. Many times as I was learning the sport, I came away from a workout on the water thinking I'd never get it and should just throw in the towel. This was precisely the time to row more, not less, and in doing so I was able to develop a reasonably respectable stroke.

The same principle applies to public speaking. More is better. Once you make the commitment to develop your speaking ability, you must seek all opportunities to speak. Some experiences will not go as you would hope, but the only way to get better is to do it. And if you've committed to a professional career, you need this skill in your toolbox alongside all of the knowledge and capabilities of your chosen profession. Some people join Toastmaster-type organizations for this purpose. Some attend public speaking classes offered commercially. While I've done neither of these, I would say that any public speaking experience adds to your skill, and if these ideas work for you, go for it.

Listening

Listening is at least half of effective communication. While it is your responsibility to foster good listening when you're speaking by being interesting, you should also accept the responsibility for listening when others are speaking. This does not come easily for some.

Listening is an art, and as with most art, almost anyone can become at least competent in its practice. And as with most interpersonal activities, effective listening starts with interest in the speaker and what's being said. It's a respect issue. Truly listening to a speaker is an affirming action that demonstrates respect for the speaker and engages him with the listener. This is really necessary for the development of a relationship, whether the speaker is subordinate, client, or senior colleague.

My own first rule of listening is to do whatever is necessary to approach the conversation with a genuine interest in the speaker and his subject. That part is usually pretty easy for me, as I imagine it would be for any reasonably curious individual. I then consciously communicate my interest in the speaker through maintaining eye contact, nodding, and giving other indications that I am listening. Then, the capstone of the effort is to question and challenge the speaker in appropriate and respectful ways. This confirms for the speaker that I'm listening and that I care enough to round out my understanding of his observations.

If the above sounds like window dressing (and at times I have to confess it may be), consider that these habits are also very conducive to learning. Sometimes I surprise myself with the amount and value of the information I have picked up in conversations in which I thought I had no interest simply because I practiced these disciplines. Try it. You'll be delighted with what you've learned at the same time that you're gaining fans for being interested in what interests them.

16

You and Your Firm

In my last year of graduate school, I was certain that I wanted to join a large public accounting firm and was almost as certain that I would be there for my entire career. But how was I to know for sure, without having experienced it? Most of my friends were in the same predicament. One, however, actually worked for one of these firms.

He was on the inside, experiencing it on a day-to-day basis. No matter that his part-time job was only inserting updates into loose-leaf binders. He knew a great deal more than the rest of us about what that world was like. He was the source of virtually all we knew about this world. It was a classic example of the old adage, "in the realm of the blind, a one-eyed man is king."

Today, many firms provide professional school students with opportunities to experience the environment before graduation through internships and short-term employment. Nevertheless, many recent professional school graduates have never before been employed in the professional world. So just how will their relationships with their new firms differ from those with employers they may have had in the past? This chapter discusses the unique relationship between a young professional and his firm—in particular the responsibilities of each to the other.

What Your Firm Owes You

Working environments differ significantly among different professions. The basic relationship between firm and staff, however, should have certain characteristics that are not unique, and that foster a working attitude of mutual respect and trust. This relationship must be founded upon an understanding by each that the other has certain needs that must be met in order for the relationship to function. Some firms and some individuals do this well.

Others don't. The key for both parties is to recognize when it is working and when it is not.

The three principal needs that you bring to the table are:

- To receive a fair level of compensation for your services;

- To have the opportunity to develop your career; and

- To be treated with respect for the professional that you are.

You should legitimately expect your firm to help you satisfy each of these needs.

Your Compensation

Compensation can be a tricky subject. It is almost universally the most highly charged issue between employer and employee. Many firms, particularly large ones, will tend to see your compensation as simply a market-value issue. They often judge the worth of an employee by the salary that it would take to replace her in the marketplace at any particular point in time.

Large firms tend to think this way simply because one individual employee is less important to them than that same employee would be to a small firm, particularly when that employee is inexperienced. They can afford to see it this way, and in fact are almost forced to. Any large employer is particularly concerned about maintaining the salary structure; that is, the parity and progression of salaries among its employees as they grow in capabilities, and the maintenance of a logical relationship between salary and responsibility levels. To have two employees at

the same level of experience, performance, and responsibility earning different salaries will almost always become
a troublesome situation. The lower compensated employee, when she finds out that her peer is earning more, will
virtually always be dissatisfied. Morale suffers. Thus,
rather than risk this situation, the larger firm will stick to
its pay scale and figure that if someone is unhappy enough
about it to leave, that person can be replaced at the indicated salary level. Hence, the pay scale itself must periodically be adjusted to reflect what similarly experienced
employees could make at comparable firms.

Thus, so the thinking goes, there is also equity in the pay
scale for the employee in the sense that if she's unhappy
about her compensation level, she can look around for
another firm. The result of this salary system, then, is that
even though the employee has a legitimate right to expect
to be fairly compensated for her work, she may not always
agree with her employer as to just exactly what "fair" is.

Compensation is also tricky for another reason.
Competitive people view their compensation as a scorecard
on how they're doing relative to their peers. Consequently,
salary expectations sometimes become difficult to meet for
employees who have particularly high opinions of themselves and their work. Ultimately, all compensation is per-
formance-based, and your view of your performance and its
value may not always agree with that of your employer.
And as a result of these factors, compensation tends to be
viewed in a very short-term context—what I am making
now, and what I will be making after my raise next month.

The only reasonable response to this circumstance, in
my opinion, is to take the long view of your worth and
consider it within the context of your overall relationship
with your employer. What does that mean? First of all, I

suggest that you periodically step back and assess this relationship in terms of all three of the needs you have as they are listed above. Consider whether you see yourself growing as a professional in the way and to the extent that you want to grow, and feel you should be growing. Consider also whether you are being genuinely treated with professional respect. Then consider what you know about the market value of your services. If you feel you are not adequately compensated, ask yourself if it is simply a problem with your most recent salary adjustment, or whether the problem has been developing over time. Likewise, you may feel that you are adequately paid, or perhaps even overcompensated, but are uncomfortable that the firm is not providing you with the opportunities that you need to grow beyond where you are. Recall what you've learned in Chapters 3 and 4 about leverage and utilization, and consider whether your firm has a critical need for you to continue performing at a level that you feel you've outgrown.

When you look at the situation within the context of all of your needs, you can then better judge how to move ahead. Remember that things are rarely perfect. If your professional capabilities are developing nicely and you're being treated with the respect that you deserve (your two non-salary needs), perhaps it's a good idea to wait out your present unhappiness over your compensation. This is not to say, however, that you need to be quiet about it. The often-overlooked step that lies between doing nothing and taking a job with another firm is to discuss your concerns with the appropriate partner or supervisor.

I've found these conversations to be quite productive throughout my career, both as the employee and as the partner. If handled appropriately, they can open up an important line of communication that will help you both in the future. First of all, you will let your firm know that there's an element of your relationship that concerns you. This can be valuable information for your employer, and may cause the firm to re-examine your current salary level. At the least, it will put the firm on notice that you are assessing all elements of your relationship. If it sees you as having a legitimate concern, then the partners will likely be especially attentive to your expectations in the next salary review. You've made your point, and if done with the proper level of respect for the firm, you've probably gained the respect of the partners in the process.

This conversation may also open the door for your employer to justify its salary decision to you. There may be factors in this determination that you were unaware of, and this will be your opportunity to learn more about the compensation process and the firm's operations and decision making. It may also provide a direct link (if one hasn't already been made clear) between your performance reviews and your compensation.

How you handle your part of this conversation is of paramount importance. You must do one thing well, and you must absolutely avoid doing another. First, be as certain as you can be of what you know and believe. Don't go on a fishing expedition, hoping that if you whine a little, you'll be given more money. Review your understanding of your performance and your professional growth. Do some homework on comparable salaries in the marketplace. Put these things together into a picture of what is an appropriate level of compensation in your view.

The thing that you must absolutely avoid doing is giving any appearance of threatening your employer. This conversation is not about your opportunities elsewhere.

This is about gaining a meeting of the minds between a respected firm and a loyal employee over that employee's performance and worth to the firm. You must begin this conversation in good faith, or it has the potential to degenerate into mistrust. If things are otherwise going well for you at your firm, sewing doubt is the last thing you want to do.

In summary, my recommendation to you is to view your compensation on a long term basis, within the context of the other important elements of your relationship. Recognize that, regardless of your employer, you will almost certainly have years when you feel that you are undercompensated, but that if things are going well for you both, any deficiency will be made up in the near future. If you have this conversation and are still concerned about the issue, or if you conclude that your other needs are not being met, then start looking seriously at your options. It may be time to move on.

Developing Your Career

Throughout your first few years in your profession, continually ask yourself where you want your career to go. Recognize that this may change. You may have every expectation when taking your first professional job of building your career in your profession, only to discover in the trenches that it just doesn't work for you. Likewise, you may leave professional school intending to put in a short few years, to get a professional license for example, only to find that you have a talent for what you are doing and want to make it your life's work. Once you have this path in view, you will be much better equipped to manage the process. Remember, you are principally responsible for your career. It's your firm's job to help, but you should be prepared help it help you when things aren't working the way they should.

The jobs your firm assigns you are its principal tool for helping you manage your career development. It supplements this by reviewing your performance and providing you with continuing education. Most people develop best when they receive a healthy mix of all three of these. If your firm is serious about helping you manage your career development, it will appreciate your input on each of these subjects.

Your perception of your professional growth is a critical element in the equation. You should test this understanding continually. To compare yourself vertically, ask yourself how your capability has grown over the past year in comparison with the skills of a favorite partner or supervisor. What does he do that you couldn't have done last year, but can do now? Is he giving you more complex assignments than at this time last year? Are you being recognized by other partners in a way that suggests they view you as an emerging talent? What have your performance reviews indicated about this, and do they reflect the thought and intellectual honesty that you can rely on to guide you?

Horizontally, ask yourself what your peers have been working on recently. Have their projects required greater skill levels than yours, or do yours indicate that your skills are equally well-respected by the partners?

Your mentor should be a mainstay for you on the question of your professional growth and development. If you have one who is doing the job with objectivity and dedication, this person should have just the right blend of experience and interest in your career to provide excellent help. It's her job to discuss your own observations and concerns about your career with you.

Professional Respect

The issue of professional respect is as much a matter of environment as it is about the way that you're treated on a day to day basis. Certainly, you want to be treated as a professional, and have a legitimate right to be. The absence of this will often indicate that you're not where you need to be for the long term. But what is meant by "professional respect"? To me, it means respect for your professional ideas and opinions, and for you as a person. Thus, it is manifested in many ways, some of which are directly related to your other needs. Let's start here.

How does your firm view its compensation commitment to you? Is this a cost to the firm that must be minimized above all other considerations? Being a professional firm's largest expense, it goes without saying that salaries must be tightly managed. But given that, does the firm reward its employees in a spirit of partnership? Does it, for example, share the harvest in good years through bonuses or profit sharing? Or does it only share the pain of bad years through meager salary adjustments? Do the partners view your compensation as a win-win, anticipating that their generosity will enhance your commitment to the firm and your professional dedication to its clients? Or do you have the distinct feeling that you must lose in order for them to win.

You can get a good read on the respect with which the firm views you through its willingness to support your professional development. Does it express this dedication regularly through a genuine concern for your assignments, so that they build upon your previous experience? Or are you finding yourself doing essentially the same thing year after year? And how has it responded to your expressions of interest in growing? Has it expressed a commitment to support you, and has it followed through on that commitment?

Another indicator of the level of respect with which the firm and particular partners hold you is how you are treated in the presence of clients, especially when a problem develops in that relationship. Are you given the role of a less experienced member of the team, or treated as a gopher and given menial tasks in front of the client? Would the client legitimately view you as someone he would feel comfortable coming to for a particular need that falls within your experience, or have you been made to look like you do only what the partner tells you?

You'll no doubt find that you are treated differently by different partners. That's only human nature. What you should be assessing, rather, is the general professional environment within the firm and how it relates to you as a young professional. Don't get too bothered if one supervisor treats you like a slave if all the others meet your criteria. He's probably that way with everyone. Ask around.

The worth of respect depends on who is offering it. Does the environment within the firm foster the sort of professionalism that you find agreeable and in sync with your own value system and beliefs about how your profession should be practiced? In short, are the people from whom you seek respect also people whom you yourself respect? If not, then their respect may carry a price that you don't want to pay.

Your Firm's Needs

Your firm comes to its relationship with you with a list of needs that in many ways is similar to yours. That is, what your firm needs from you includes:

- The compensation of benefiting from the quality and quantity of the professional services that you provide in exchange for your salary;

- The professional growth of you helping it to become better in its marketplace and its profession; and

- Your respect, which is in many ways more complex than the related need of yours.

The Value of Your Work

You have a business relationship with your employer that stands shoulder-to-shoulder with your professional relationship. A business relationship thrives on the quality and quantity of the services provided as well as all of the intangible elements of the exchange such as timeliness, personal attentiveness, etc. This is the basis upon which your employer will judge the success of its relationship with you, and it will judge it in two arenas. The first of these is within it own offices; the second relates to how well you take care of its clients.

Depending upon your profession, a good deal of the work for the client is done within the firm's offices, not the client's. Thus your partners will have the day-to-day opportunity to observe how well you are satisfying their need for value in the services you perform.

However important this element, the way that the client perceives you is at least equally important. The client is paying for your services as well. Not directly, of course, but in its own way even more acutely felt. Professional fees can be staggering. Your client is reminded of this every time he writes a check to your firm for its services. I've found over the years that clients are usually not bashful about offering an opinion on the performance of the firm's personnel. Often this opinion is very positive, and there are few experiences in professional life as sweet as learning that your firm has received an attaboy with your name on it. But I've also had the other experience of a client coming to me with a complaint about a staff person, often asking that the offending individual be removed from the project. This obviously colors the firm's view of the staff member, even if the client's complaint makes little sense. The harsh reality is that part of being a professional in business is serving clients in such a way that they want to continue being clients. Justified or not, complaints such as this reflect negatively on the firm's good relationship with its client.

Your Firm's Growth

Your firm's need for you to help it grow is much less tangible, but probably far more important to your longer term opportunity. This often has to do with its growth in size, but perhaps more importantly with its continued ability to maintain and enhance its relevance and its competitive edge. As you know by now, each of the professions continually evolves and matures within itself. Client needs change. Rules of the profession evolve in sometimes unpredictable ways. A legislative decision can create an immediate need for re-education and re-evaluation of service needs and opportunities. In order to maintain your relevance, you must help your firm maintain its relevance within the community. You can establish yourself as a leader by placing yourself at the forefront of this evolution. Have you processed, and then led others to process, the impact of these changes on specific clients? Are your ideas contributing to the identification of new service opportunities?

But there's a still more intangible way that you affect your firm. How do you speak of your firm when there's no partner within earshot? How do your closest personal friends view your firm as a result of their conversations with you? Do you advocate for your firm without being prompted to do so? The long-term effects of this basic attitude will have a lot to do with how you will someday help the firm add to its client base. Your offhand comments about the firm are heard by others and remembered—not the specific comments perhaps, but the essence of them, I can assure you. They leave an impression that can survive for a long time. Put that together with the fact that your contemporaries, the ones to whom you are making those comments today, will someday be decision makers and buyers of professional services. What impression will they retain about your firm from hearing your comments about it? Your firm expects that any negative issues that you have with it will be discussed inside the office and resolved, and that your casual conversation with your friends will reflect positively on it. I have believed for years that negative comments about others, particularly others whom you are close to in life, reflect more negatively on the speaker than on the subject. If you buy that view, then a desire to maintain your friends' positive views of you is reason enough to at least restrict your negative comments, even if you choose to not offer any positive ones.

Your Respect for Your Firm

Respect is a two-way street, and very much a product of its environment, I've found. Whether the environment breeds respect or whether an inherent respect among individuals is somehow perpetuated by the environment is an imponder-

able. It works both ways, I think. Each supports the other.
Your role in this process is to be certain you are adding to
the professional respect your firm garners, and not detract-
ing from it. This relates not only to how you portray the
firm among your friends, but also to how you handle relationships up and down the organization chart internally. I
truly believe that the finest all-around professionals I've
know over the years were people who treated everyone they
worked with, from the receptionist to the senior partner,
with the same level of personal respect. And I believe
there's a logical explanation for this. It takes a certain level
of self-assurance to be continually mindful of the individu-
ality of and contribution made by everyone in the office.
People with this trait of civility and deference to the personalities and peculiarities of everyone in their environment project a self-confidence in themselves as contributors
as well. Perhaps the way we treat others is simply a reflection of our own professional respect for ourselves.

17

In Conclusion

Now you've acquired the education to create a great professional career for yourself. It's what you've worked so hard and long to gain. And the knowledge you've gained is yours for good. Only your own inattention to maintaining it can diminish its value to you and to others.

What you've read in this book can be your launching pad for that career. You've learned how professional firms work and a lot about how their partners think and act. You're undoubtedly thinking about how you fit into that environment and what you will have to do to succeed. But the knowledge you've gained here must be maintained as well. Test my experiences and observations against your own. Shape what you've learned here against the real world as you find it. Decide how you see the issues I've presented and what works and what doesn't in your own firm and situation.

As you gain your own experiences and beliefs about success in the professional world, please share them with me. I commit to you that I will do two things:

- I will keep your identity and specific comments confidential; and

- I will do my best to integrate your experiences and observations with my own and share them for the benefit of readers of subsequent editions of this book.

You can do this by visiting www.windrosepress.com and clicking on "Your Thoughts".

Now, I offer you my best wishes for a long and successful professional career and the rich rewards that flow from it!

For More Information

Block, Peter, *Flawless Consulting: A Guide to Getting Your Expertise Used*, 2nd edition, San Francisco: Jossey-Bass/Pfeiffer, 2000.

> When the first edition of this book was recom-
> mended to me by a fellow consultant years ago,
> he said of it, "Every time I screw up in any
> part of my practice, I go home, pick up
> *Flawless Consulting* and find what I did wrong."
> I've had this experience too.

Covey, Stephen R., *The 7 Habits of Highly Effective People: Restoring the Character Ethic*, New York: Simon & Schuster, 1989.

> This book, out of all the others on the subject
> of managing your life, has made the most sense
> to me since I first read it shortly after it was
> published. Covey is great in helping readers to
> see the issues of balance and priorities as they
> really are.

Maister, David H., *True Professionalism: The Courage to Care About Your People, Your Clients, and Your Career*, New York: Touchstone, 1997.

> Maister's book treats some of the same material as I have, but more from the viewpoint of an established practitioner. It is a worthwhile read for another perspective on the areas where we overlap as well as some issues you'll face later in your career.

Windrose Press
A division of Orion Group, LLC

Order Additional Copies of *Professional Success*

Internet: Please visit www.windrosepress.com—Instructions are online

Fax: 650.595.2232—Use this form with your credit card information

Mail: Windrose Press, PO Box 790, San Carlos, CA 94070—
Send this form with your check or credit card information

Telephone: 650.595.2550—Have your credit card ready

Please send *Professional Success: How to Thrive in the Professional World*
to the following address immediately:

Name: _____

Address: _____

City: _____ State: _____ Zip Code: _____

Telephone: _____ email: _____

Professional Success _____ copies @ $18.95 = $ _____

Sales Tax (for shipments within California)   7.25% = $ _____

Shipping and Handling
$4.00 per copy in U.S., $ 9.00 per copy international $ _____

TOTAL ORDER   = $ _____

Payment by:

☐ Enclosed Check or Money Order

Credit Card   ☐ VISA   ☐ Master Card   ☐ Optima
☐ American Express   ☐ Discover

Card Number: _____

Expiration Date: _____

Name on Card _____

Address on Card (if different from above)

_____

_____

_____